The Prisoner of Mainz

GW01464205

Alec Waugh

Alpha Editions

This edition published in 2024

ISBN 9789362516831

Design and Setting By
Alpha Editions
www.alphaedis.com
Email - info@alphaedis.com

Contents

CHAPTER I

THE GREAT OFFENSIVE

§ 1

March 21st, 1918.

THE small box respirator, like the thirty-nine articles of the Faith, should be taken on trust; one is quite prepared to believe in its efficiency. Countless Base instructors have extolled it, countless memos from Division have confirmed their panegyrics; and with these credentials one carries it on one's chest in a perfect faith; but one has no wish to put its merits to the test. No one if he can help it wishes to have his face surrounded by elastic and india-rubber, and his nose clamped viciously by bent iron; and for that reason my chief memory of March 21st was the prolonged discomfort of a gas-mask.

For from the moment that the barrage opened at 5 a.m. the air was full of the insidious smell of gas. Masks were clapped on, and thus hooded the machine-gunners fumbled desperately in search of stoppages; it was an uncomfortable morning.

Being stationed about two miles north of the left flank of the German attack, it was for us a much more comfortable morning than that spent by most of those south of Arras. For when the mist began to rise, it revealed no phantom figures; we did not find ourselves encircled, and outflanked, with the cheerful alternatives of a perpetual rest where we stood or of an indefinite sojourn on the wrong side of the line. Everything presented a very orderly appearance. Far away on the right was the dull noise of guns, but over the whole of the immediate front spread out the peaceful prospect of a programme of trench routine.

"Seems as if Jerry weren't coming over after all," said the section corporal.

"Looks like it," I said.

"Then I suppose as we'd better clean things up a bit, Sir."

"It would be as well."

And the half-section settled down to the usual work of cleaning themselves, their guns, and their position. The infantry on the right were even more resigned to the uneventful.

"This 'ere offensive was all wind up, Sir," said the man at the strombos form, "they thought we was gettin' a bit slack, I suppose, so they thought this scare 'ud smarten us up a bit; but I knew it all along, Sir; I'm too old a soldier to be taken in by that."

The runner from Battalion, however, brought quite a different story.

"Been an attack all along the line, Arras to St. Quentin, but it's been broken up absolutely; never even got the front line."

The man at the strombos form shifted suspiciously.

"They not bin trying to come over 'ere. I never seen no Germans," which was not surprising considering that from where he stood he could not see the front line at all.

"No," he went on, "there's bin no offensive, and there won't be one neither. It's all a wind up."

At any rate, whether there had been an attempted attack or not, it seemed quite clear that it had not got very far. With that comforting certainty, I returned to the position, and having seen that the guns were clean, descended into the dugout and went to sleep.

About two hours later a perspiring runner arrived. He was quite out of breath from dodging whizzbangs, and was in consequence incapable of logical statement. He said something about "Bullecourt." The chit he brought explained.

"BULLECOURT, ECOUST, NOREIL ARE IN THE
HANDS OF THE ENEMY"

It took at least five minutes to realise what this meant. To think that they had got as far as that. It had seemed so delightfully safe. One had walked along the Ecoust road in daylight, and there was a canteen at Noreil. And then that glorious dugout in Railway Reserve that we had covered with green canvas and festooned with semi-nudities from the *Tatler*, to think of some lordly Prussian straddling across the table, swigging champagne. It was an unspeakable liberty....

And then a little tardily followed the thought that Ecoust was not so many miles from Monchy, and that if the Germans had got as far as that on the right, there was very little reason why they should not do the same to us—an unpleasant consideration. But still everything seemed so delightfully quiet. Only an occasional whizzbang, or four—five—no one would have thought there was a war on. Still Ecoust was not so very far off; our parish had provided funds for a church army hut at St. Leger. They had been collecting for it hard when I had been on leave. Well, that must have gone west by now....

And at the top of the dugout I could hear the runner gradually recovering his breath and explaining the strategic situation in spasms.

"You see, I heard the captin say to the adjutant, 'Jones,' he says, 'the Jerrys' got as far as Bullecourt,' and when I heard that ... well ... I said to myself ... thank 'eavens I wasn't there."

"And you was there two months ago, Kid."

"Where I was two months ago, as you say, and then I heard the captin say...."

The remaining reflection was inaudible.

The next morning passed very quietly, so quietly that we had almost forgotten the rumours of the preceding day. The limber corporal had assured the ration party that there had been a counter-attack with tanks, and that not only had Bullecourt been retaken, but Hendecourt and Riencourt as well. There seemed no cause for panic. The rum had come up as usual, and that was the main thing. After an afternoon of belt-cleaning the subsection arranged itself as usual into night reliefs, and then just before midnight came the news that the Division was evacuating to the "third" line.

Whenever the military decide on a sudden action, they impart the information in a delightfully inconsequent way. For instance, on the eve of the Cambrai show, orders were sent round that in the case of an enemy withdrawal limbers would proceed to Hendecourt along the road in the map square U 29 B, and this request was then qualified by the statement, "It is no good looking for roads; there are none."

On this occasion the message was equally vague. It stated that the front system would be evacuated at 3 a.m., and ordered that all guns, tripods, belt-boxes, and ammunition would be immediately moved and stacked at the ration dump pending the arrival of limbers. The chit then added, "Secrecy is absolutely essential. On no account must the men know anything of this." The reasons on which the authorities based their expectations that the men would move all their impedimenta to a ration dump, and yet remain in complete ignorance of the operation, are unfathomable. At any rate their hopes were unrealised. At the first mention of dismounted guns, Private Hawkins had sniffed the secret.

"Got to shift, 'ave we, Sir? Then I suppose we're going to have a war too, aren't we, Sir?"

"I should not be surprised," I told him, and went below to superintend the packing of my kit. It was no easy matter. Things accumulate in the line; I always went up the line with a modestly filled pack, but by the time I came down, it needed a mailbag to hold the books and magazines that had gradually gathered round me, and after a fortnight in the same dugout my kit was in no condition for emergency transportation.

My batman was examining it with a sorrowful face.

"You'll 'ave to dump most of these books, Sir."

"Oh, but surely we can get some of them down?"

"Then you'll have to dump those boots, Sir, and that blanket. Can't take the lot, Sir."

It was no use to argue with him. The batman's orders are far more law than a mandate from Brigade. The Brigadier is merely content to issue orders; batmen see that theirs are carried out. There was nothing for it but to dump the books, and I looked sadly at the considerable collection that the mails of the last fourteen days had brought.

"Have they all got to go?"

"'Fraid so, Sir."

"What, all my pretty chickens, at one fell swoop?"

Private Warren eyed me stolidly.

"Well, Sir, I might manage two, Sir, but no more."

I ran a pathetic eye over them. There were several I particularly wanted to save; there were two novels by Hardy, Robert Graves's new book of Poems, *Regiment of Women*, a battered copy of *La Terre*, *The Oxford Book of Verse*, *The Stucco House*. After a moment's hesitation, the last two were saved for further odysseys; there was just room in a spare pocket for *Fairies and Fusiliers*; the rest would have to stay to welcome the Teuton.

At last all the equipment of a machine-gun section had been carted away. I took one turn round the dugouts to see that no incriminating document remained. The dugout looked hospitably clean; all the delicacies of handing over had been observed, but as there would be up one to receive the relieving party, manners demanded some sort of "Salve"; and so, tearing from a notebook a sheet of paper, I scrawled across it in large letters, CHEERIOH, and pinned it over the entrance of my deserted home.

§ 2

March 28th, 1918.

Of course the limbers never turned up. For two months without the least inconvenience from German artillery they had come up to the ration dump every night, but on this particular night they felt sure it would arouse suspicions, and so a guide was sent instead. And in France there are only two sorts of guides. There is the guide who does not know the way and owns up to it, and there is the guide who does not know the way and pretends he does. There are no others. Luckily ours came under the former category.

"You see, Sir, I've only bin from Headquarters once and that was by day, and I'm not too sure of the way…. I've only been 'ere once and that…."

Which was a pretty clear sign that a compass bearing would be hardly less reliable. We dumped most of our spare kit in the river, and set off. It is wonderful how disorderly any movement of troops appears by night. Actually it was a most methodical withdrawal, but in its progress it looked pitifully like a rout. The road seemed littered with cast-off equipment, ammunition, packs and bombs; dumps were going up all round. Innumerable Highlanders had lost their companies; nobody seemed to know where he was going or to care particularly whether he ever arrived. A subsection of fifteen men straggled into an echelon formation covering as many yards. It appeared an absolute certainty that dawn and the Germans would find us still trailing helplessly along the road.

At last, however, came the loved jingle of harness, and the sound of restive mules. We heaved packs and baggages on a limber, and more cheerfully resumed our odyssey.

This cheerfulness considerably diminished when the section found that our new positions were two hundred yards from the road, and that a hundred boxes of S.A.A. had to be stacked in half an hour. But eventually peace was restored to Israel, and by the time that the morning broke, the section was fairly comfortably lodged in some disused German dugouts.

There followed four very lazy days. The two subsections had been amalgamated, and with my section officer Evans, I spent most of the day working out elaborate barrage charts in case of a break through. Evans had recently been on a course at Camières where they had given him an enormous blue sheet which was warranted proof against geography. Evans regarded it as a sort of charm.

"You see, with this," he said, "you can get on to any target you like within thirty seconds."

And it was certainly an ingenious toy, but as far as we were concerned, it did not accelerate the conclusion of the war. It required a level table, numerous drawing-pins, carbon papers, faultless draughtsmanship and much else with which we were unequipped: finally, when occasion demanded we resorted to the obsolete method of aiming at the required target.

Of the actual war little information was gleaned. The limber corporal brought each evening the account of wondrous sallies and excursions. Lens was purported to have fallen, and an enveloping attack was in progress further North. Lille was only a matter of days. And then on the night of the 27th there arrived the mail and papers of the preceding seven days. It came in an enormous burst of epistolary shrapnel. Personally I received thirty letters and five parcels. We sat up reading them till midnight, and then in a contented frame of mind we turned to the papers. It was a bit of a shock. We had hardly imagined that there was a war on any front except our own. We had expected to see headlines talking of nothing but the Fall of Bullecourt and our masterly evacuation of Monchy. We had expected to see our exploits extolled by Philip Gibbs; instead of that they filled a very insignificant corner. It was all Bapaume, Ham, Peronne. We were merely a false splash of a wave that already had gone home. It was a blow to our self-respect. There was also no news of any enveloping manœuvres round Lille. The Germans appeared to be doing all that.

Evans looked across at me dolefully.

"Do you think the men had better know anything about that?" he said.

"Shouldn't think so. By the way, when are we being relieved?"

"The sooner the better. There is going to be a war on soon."

And the memory of the thirty letters and five parcels thinned.

"Oh, well," I said, "I'm going to bed."

My sleep did not last long. Within an hour Evans was shouting in my ear.

"Hell of a strafe upstairs. I think they're coming over."

And indeed there was a strafe. Verey lights were going up all along the front. Three dumps were hit in as many minutes, from the right came the continual crump of "minnies." Luckily we were in the shelter between the barrage on the eighteen-pounders and the barrage on the front lines. The only shells that came disconcertingly close were those from one of our own heavies that was dropping short, like a man out of breath.

At seven o'clock the Germans came over, and by twelve we were being escorted to Berlin.

Our actual engagement resembles so closely that of every other unfortunate during those sorry days that it deserves no detailed description. The only original incident came at about nine o'clock when I discovered the perfidy of the section cook. I had sent him down to fetch some breakfast, and he returned smoking triumphantly a gold-tipped cigarette that he could have obtained from only one source. Perhaps this is what those mean who maintain that in the moment of action one sees the naked truth of the human soul. At any rate it stripped Private Hawkins pretty effectively. No doubt this kleptomania had been a practice with him for a long time, and at this critical moment I suppose he saw no reason why he should conceal it: "much is forgiven to a man condemned." He literally flaunted theft.

"AT SEVEN O'CLOCK THE GERMANS CAME OVER."
[To face page 16.

"Hawkins," I said quietly, "you'll go back to the gun-team to-morrow. We'll find another cook."

"Very good, Sir."

And almost instantly the order was given a divine confirmation in the form of the cushiest of flesh wounds in Private Hawkins's right arm.

After a second's gasp he bounded down the trench.

"A blighty, Sir," he cried, "a blighty. No, Sir, don't want to be bound up or anything. They'll do that at the dressing station. I'm orf."

Visions had risen before him of white sheets and whiter nurses. He saw himself being petted and made much of, the hero of the village; and as the Germans slowly filtered round the flank, Private Hawkins rushed down the communication trench, resolved to put at all cost the dressing station between them and him. He succeeded. Probably it was the one time he had ever tried to do anything in his life.

CHAPTER II

ON THE WAY TO THE RHINE

§ 1

AT the back of the mind there always exists a sort of unconscious conception of the various contingencies that may lie round the corner. It is usually unformulated, but it is there none the less, and at the moment when I was captured I had a very real if confused idea of what was going to happen to me.

The idea was naturally confused because the etiquette of surrender is not included in Field Service Regulations, and as it is not with that intention that one originally sets out for France, the matter had not bulked largely in the imagination. But the terrorist had supplied these deficiencies, and he had made it hard to rid oneself of the supposition that one had only to cross a few yards of unowned hollows to find oneself in a world of new values and formulæ. As a dim recollection of some previous existence I had carried the image of strange brutalities and assaults, of callous, domineering Prussians, of Brigadiers with Sadistic temperament. I was fully prepared to be relieved of my watch and cigarette-case, and to be prodded in the back by my escort's bayonet.

Instead of that, however, he presented me with a cigar and pretended to understand my French, which is on the whole the most insidious of all forms of compliment.

There was also a complete absence of that machine-perfect discipline of which we had heard so much. Several of the German officers had not shaved, men stood to the salute with their heels wide apart, and the arrival of a silver epaulette was not the sign for any Oriental prostrations. Beyond the fact that the men wore grey uniforms and smoked ungainly pipes, they strangely resembled an English battalion that was carrying on a minor local engagement.

The authorities who interviewed us and confiscated our correspondence displayed the characteristic magnanimity of the captor; after enlarging on the individual merits of the Entente soldier, they proceeded to explain why they themselves were winning the war.

"It's staff work that counts," they said. "We've got unity of command; Hindenburg. You've got two generals, Haig and Foch."

Indeed, everywhere behind the line there was intense gratification, but not so much of the victory-lust that must have inflamed them in the early months of the war, but of the weariness that four years had brought, and of the thought that the close of so much misery was near. Actual successes (so it appeared) were only the means to an end—it was peace that mattered.

All this was very different from what I had expected. On the way to Battalion Headquarters I had visioned an inquisitional cross-examination. I had expected to be questioned by some fierce-jawed general, who would demand the secrets of the General Staff, which I should heroically refuse. Then he would call for the thumbscrew and the rack, for the cat-o'-nine-tails and the red-hot iron. "Will you speak now?" he would hiss. But I should remain as ever steadfastly loyal. The entire scenic panorama of the *Private of the Buffs* had swept before my eye; only a spasm of optimism had changed the crisis. Just at the moment when I was being led out to be shot, the general would suddenly relent. His voice would shake, and a quiver would run down his massive frame.

"No, no!" he would say, with out-stretched hand. "Spare him! He's only a boy, and besides he's a soldier and, damn it! that's all that I am myself."

Actuality, however, refused to reflect the Lyceum stage. The man with the records viewed my presence with complete equanimity.

"Oh, well," he said, "it's no good my asking you any questions. You'd be sure to answer them wrong, and besides, I don't think you could tell me so very much. Let's see, you're in the —— Division, aren't you? Well, you've got the following battalions with you."

And he proceeded to give gratuitous information on the most intricate points of organisation and establishment, all the hundred and one little things that had been so laboriously tabulated before the Sandhurst exams., and had afterwards been so speedily forgotten. He knew the number of stretcher-bearers in a battalion, the number of G.S. wagons at brigade, and the quantity of red tabs at division. Any one possessing a quarter of his knowledge could have had a staff appointment for the asking.

"Not bad," he laughed.

It was now two o'clock in the afternoon, and since the barrage had opened at three in the morning, none of us had sat down for a moment. We began to entertain hopes of lunch.

"Where are we bound for?" I asked.

"Douai."

"But we don't march there to-day, do we?"

"If you can," he said cheerfully. "But it's about twenty kilos, and by the time you've got to Vitry you probably won't be sorry to have a rest."

The prospect of a twenty-kilometre march along the unspeakable French roads was anything but encouraging. It was drizzling slightly, and there seemed no likelihood of getting any food. In a sad silence we waited, while the scattered groups of prisoners were collected into a party sufficiently large to be moved off together.

Proceedings were at this point considerably delayed by a company sergeant-major of the Blankshires who had spent his last moments of liberty near the rum jar; and under its influence he could not rid himself of the idea that he was still in charge of a parade. Nothing would induce him to fall in in the ranks. He persisted in standing on a bank, from which he directed operations in bucolic spasms, meanwhile treating the Germans with the benevolent patronage that he had been wont to display before the newly-joined subaltern. It was the one flash of humour that that grey afternoon provided.

At last enough stragglers had dribbled in, six officers and about a hundred and twenty men, and the march back began.

Nothing could exceed the depression of that evening. The rain began to fall heavily, and through its dim sheets peered the mournful eyes of ruined villages. We marched in silence; Vis-en-Artois, Dury, Torquennes, one by one they were passed, the landmarks we had once picked out from the Monchy heights. A stage of exhaustion had been reached when movement became mechanical. For twelve hours we had had no food, and no rest for at least sixteen, and to this physical weariness was added the depression that the bleak French landscape never fails to evoke—the grey stretches of rolling ground unrelieved by colour; the dead-straight roads lined by tree-stumps, the broken homesteads; and to all this was again added the cumulative helplessness that the events of the day had roused; the knowledge of the ignominy of one's position, and the uncertainty of what was to come.

Gradually the succession of broken houses yielded to whole but deserted villages; and these woke even more the sense of loneliness, of nostalgia. Formerly, on the way back from the line, there was nothing so cheering as to see through the night the first signs of civilisation. Then they were to the imagination as kindly hands welcoming it back to the joys from which it had been exiled. But now the shadowy arms of a distant windmill only served to increase the feeling of banishment and separation. Behind us we could hear the dull roll of guns, we could see the flares of the Verey lights curving against the sky; and these seemed nearer happiness than the untouched barns.

At last towards ten o'clock we reached Vitry and were herded into an open cage. The whole surface of it was a liquid slime, round which men were moving, trying to keep warm. Sleep there was impossible. But at any rate there was something to eat, a cup of coffee, a quarter of a loaf of bread. The German officer received us as a hotel-keeper receives guests for whom he has no beds.

"I am very sorry, gentlemen," he said; "but you're only here for one night. But I think I might be able to find you a little room in the hut for the wounded."

And so tired were we that there was pleasure in the mere prospect of a roof; and on a floor covered with lousy straw we passed the night in snatches of sleep, disturbed every moment by the tossing of cramped limbs, and by the presence of muddy boots driven against one's face, and brawny Highlanders sprawling across one's chest. But in that state of exhaustion these troubles were remote—for a while at any rate we could be still; and in the waking moments there lay no venom even in the recurring thought that on the next morning we should have to begin our march afresh.

§ 2

At Douai we spent four days of incorrigible prolixity in a small house behind the bank. There was absolutely nothing to do. We had no books: we could not write. There was no chess-board, and the only pack of cards was two aces short. All we could do was to sleep spasmodically, and try not to remember that we were hungry.

It was an impossible task. There was nothing else to think about. There was no chance of forgetting how little we had had for breakfast. Slowly we dragged from meal to meal.

For breakfast we got a cup of coffee made from chestnuts, and an eighth of a loaf of bread. For lunch there was a bowl of vegetable soup. For supper another cup of coffee, and another eighth of a loaf. Each morning there was an infinitesimal issue of jam. That comprised our entire ration.

We also had nothing to smoke.

There was nothing for it but to lie on our beds, with every road of thought leading to the same gate. One remembered the most minute details of dinners enjoyed on leave. A steaming array of visionary dishes passed continually before the eyes. One thought of the tins of unwanted bully stacked at the foot of dugouts. And for myself there was the bitter recollection of three untouched parcels that I had received on the eve of capture.

"To think of it," I said, "a whole haggis, two cakes, four tins of salmon!"

"Appalling!" echoed the others.

"And to think that the Jerrys have got it!"

"Don't talk about it, man; let's forget."

But there was no escape.

"As a perfume doth remain
In the folds where it hath lain,"

so lingered the thoughts of those untouched delicacies.

The only interesting features of our day were the talks we had with one of the German interpreters. It was the first time that any of us had a chance of discovering their attitude towards the Entente, and it was interesting to see how closely their propaganda had followed our own lines.

To our accounts of atrocities in Belgium, the Germans had retorted with stories about the Russian invasion of East Prussia. By them the employment of native troops against white men was represented as an offence against humanity as gross as the use of gas. Nothing, moreover, would shake their belief that France and Russia were the aggressors. To the interpreter it was a war of self-defence. There is no doubt that his faith in this was absolutely sincere.

But what really touched him most closely was the propaganda of our Press.

"Surely you cannot believe," he said, "that we are an entire nation of barbarians? Whatever our quarrels, you surely ought to allow that we are human beings. If it had not been for your newspaper chiefs," he added, "the war would have been over in 1916."

It was the one point on which he was really bitter.

One morning we were standing in the courtyard, and a German orderly was chopping up wood for our fires. It was a bit cold, and to keep himself warm one of the officers went over to help him.

The interpreter turned to the rest of us and said: "Now then, if your *John Bull* could get hold of a photograph of that, he'd print huge headlines, 'Ill-treatment of British Officers. Made to chop up wood for German soldiers.'"

It was at Douai that we discovered for the first time the German habit of putting dictaphones in prisoners' rooms. Ours was attached to the electric light appliances and masqueraded as a switch wire. But if any one listened to our conversation, they can have heard very little to interest them, save perhaps sundry strings of unsavoury epithets preceding the word "Boche."

From Douai we moved to Marchiennes; half of the way by tram. Every time we stopped, French women crowded round us bringing cigarettes and tobacco.

"It is not allowed," said the German sergeant-major, "but I shall be blind."

Material comforts were even fewer at our new resting-place. There were eight of us and we were put in a large, draughty barn, with bed-boards covered with bracken that was unspeakably lousy. There were no rugs or blankets of any description, and the nights were miserably cold. The eight days we spent there were the worst of our whole captivity. The food, consisting mainly of a stew of bad fish and sauerkraut, was at times uneatable. Indeed, things would have gone very badly with us, had we not managed to make friends with one of our guard. He was very small and very grubby, and introduced himself to us one morning when the commandant was not about.

"Me Alsacian," he said. "English, French, kamarades. Prussians, ugh! nix."

From this basis of common sympathies negotiations proceeded as smoothly as linguistic difficulties permitted. He told us that, if we wanted food, the only way was to apply to the Maire. He himself would carry the letter.

Two hours later he returned with a loaf of bread and a packet of lard. It seemed a banquet, and for the rest of our stay he brought us, if not a living, at any rate an existing ration, and on the day that we moved he even came on to the station carrying a sack of provisions.

Our train journey provided an admirable example of official negligences. For officialdom is the same all the world over. In England it was like a game of "Old Maid"; and so it was here. To the commandant at Marchiennes eight prisoners were only so many cards to be got rid of as quickly as possible. As soon as they had been put in a train, and the requisite number of buff sheets dispatched, his job was at an end. What happened in the course of transmission mattered not at all.

And so the eight of us, with two German sentries, were put in a train at Marchiennes at ten o'clock on a Monday morning. We had rations for one day, and we reached Karlsruhe, our destination, at 7 p.m. on the Thursday. In this respect our experience is that of every other prisoner that I have met; only we, by being a small party, fared better than most.

First of all, in regard to our sentries. As there were so few of us, we soon managed to get on friendly terms with them. They were a delightful couple. One of them was medically unfit, and had never been in the trenches. He was mortally afraid of his own rifle, and at the first opportunity unloaded it. The responsibility of a live round in the breech was too great.

The other was old and kindly, with the Iron Cross; and like all men who have seen war, loathed it thoroughly.

"Englander and German," he said, "trenches, ah, blutig; capout; here alles kameraden; krieg, nix mehr."

And at every station he tried to get food out of the authorities. He was not very successful. Only once, at Louvain, did he manage to raise some bully beef and bread, and if we had had to rely on official largess, we should have been very thin by the time we reached Karlsruhe. But luckily, through being a small party, we were able to benefit from the generosity of the Belgian civilians at a small village called Bout-Merveille, who showered on us bread and eggs and cigarettes.

But for all that the journey was tedious beyond words. We were crowded in a third-class carriage, with unpadded seats. We had nothing to read. Wherever the train stopped at a siding it remained there for any period from four to seven hours; it did all its movement by night, and for at least ten hours of daylight presented us with a stationary landscape. It seemed as though it would never end. Nor did our arrival in Germany afford any diversion. Another traditional conception "went west." We had all vaguely expected to receive some insult or brutality at the hands of the civilian population. But no old men spat on us, no hectic women attacked us with their hair-pins. Instead of that they regarded us with a friendly curiosity.

"Cheer up!" one girl said to us. "The war'll soon be over. You will be back in four months."

It was the same here as behind the line. Peace—nothing else mattered. The Germans had suffered so much personally that they had ceased to nourish the collective loyalties of world power and empire. They no longer wanted to conquer the world, they wanted to be at peace; and to this end their victories in the field seemed the shortest way. The short snatches of conversation that we had with civilians on Heidelberg Station were all in this key. Peace would come in four months. Beyond that they had no ambitions. They no longer shared the megalomania of their rulers.

CHAPTER III

KARLSRUHE AND MILTON HAYES

AFTER the discomforts of the trenches and the tedium of a fortnight's travelling, Karlsruhe provided a delightful haven. Here all the material needs were satisfied; there was a Red Cross issue of tin foods three times a week: the beds were moderately comfortable, and one's clothes could be disinfected: and there was a library. After a fortnight's exile from books there is no joy comparable to the sight of a printed page.

And in the evenings we were allowed out till eleven o'clock. There were big arc lamps under the trees, and in this romantic atmosphere the greater part of the camp lay out reading in deck chairs. It was easy then to cast a false glamour over imprisonment; to see in it a succession of harmonious days; a quiet backwater in which the mind was free to work. It was easy to bathe the emotions in the ordered periods of George Moore's prose, and reflect that there "lay no troublous thing before." It was the reaction natural after the turgid experiences of the last eight months, and it certainly made that one week at Karlsruhe lyrical with content.

Karlsruhe was a distributing station through which all officer prisoners passed on their way to permanent camps. But there was always retained a small committee of officers to superintend the activities of this fluid community. There were officers to look after the issue of relief parcels, to run the library, to control general discipline. In charge of the Red Cross Committee was Tarrant.

Fourteen months of captivity had not made much impression either on his cheerfulness or on his health. In fact he looked and felt so fit that it caused him some alarm.

"I'm too well," he said, "I'm thinking of trying a fast."

"He's been saying that every day for the last month," remarked Stone, his room companion.

"Oh, no, old man, really," protested Tarrant, "I've only been waiting for it to get a bit warmer."

After the wearisome discussions about the incidental aspects of the war, it was an enormous delight to meet two people to whom the events of the last year had been a matter chiefly of conjecture and report.

"You will get awfully sick of all this, of course, after fourteen months," said Tarrant, "but it's really a capital place to get one's ideas settled."

One is always extraordinarily polite to a person one meets for the first time. After three days the need for politeness goes. But on that first occasion the opinions of the other are treated with a laborious respect. Conversation takes a turn of, "Of course that's quite true, but I must say that personally ..." and that was the way that Tarrant listened to my heresies on the first evening. Long before I had vanished from Karlsruhe, however, the respectful tone had degenerated into, "Won't do, old man, won't do," and there have been times since, when I have emerged sadly tattered from some war of dialectic, that I have longed wistfully for those early days.

The next afternoon Tarrant was in a chastened mood.

"I've begun my fast," he explained. "It was not so bad after breakfast. But by lunch time it got pretty awful, and by now...."

"It gets better after the third day, I'm told," Stone hazarded.

"You know," Tarrant went on, "before I began this fast, I made a whole pile of arguments in favour of it; but really at this moment, I can't remember a single one."

"Shall I suggest a few?" said Stone.

"No, thanks."

However, the resolution held good, and for the space of five complete days he did not eat a morsel of food. The moment it was over he declared it to be a capital scheme, and recommended it to all his friends.

It was at Karlsruhe that I met Milton Hayes. Off the stage he is in appearance very much like the remainder of humanity, but no one who has met him once could ever forget him. He is the one man who has accepted Popular Taste as a constant thing, has defined that thing, and found a theory on which to work.

The majority of popular artists always adopt an attitude of, "Well, there must be something about my stuff, I don't know what it is, a little trick, something that hits the popular fancy. I can't explain it."

But Milton Hayes has his theory cut and dried. He has formed a vessel in which all his work can take shape. He has written two monologues, *The Green Eye of the Little Yellow God*, and *The Whitest Man I Know*, that have sold more than any other similar compositions, and he wrote them both, as it were, to scale.

"The great thing," he said, "is to appeal to the imagination. Don't describe: suggest. All the best effects are got by placing the vital incident off the stage. Let your public imagine, don't tell them anything; just strike chords. It's no good describing a house; the person will always fix the scene in some spot that he himself knows. In as few words as possible you've got to recall that spot to him. He'll do the rest."

About the "Green Eye" he made no pretence. He wove round it no air of mystery and cracker tinsel.

"It took me five hours to write," he said, "but I worked it all out first. I don't say it's real poetry; but it does what I set out to do. It appeals to the imagination. It starts off with colours, green and yellow, that at once introduce an atmosphere. Then India: well, every one's got his idea of India; it's a symbol. It conveys something very definite to the average mind. Then play on the susceptibilities. 'His name was mad Karou': you've got the whole man. The public will fill in the picture for you. And then the mystery parts; just leave enough unsaid to make paterfamilias pat himself on the back. 'I've spotted it, he can't do me. I'm up to that dodge; I know where he went'; and when you are at the end you come back to the point you started from. It carries people back. You've got a compact whole: and you touch the sense of pathos, 'A broken-hearted woman tends the grave of mad Karou.' They'll weave a whole story round that woman's life. Every man's a novelist at heart. We all tell ourselves stories. And that's what you've got to play on."

And that is where, I think, Milton Hayes's greatness really lies. He thoroughly understands his audience; he can change places with each individual that is listening to him. He never has to try a thing on some one first to see whether it will go. He knows at once what will get over and what will not. One of the most amusing sketches he has done was a burlesque of a war-lecture made by a famous London journalist. He mimicked his subject completely, but where the real "punch" lay was in his analysis of the emotions of each individual and couple leaving the hall. He knew exactly what each one would make of it.

One of his chief maxims, too, is that an actor must remember that he is performing not to individuals but to couples.

"People don't go to shows by themselves," he said, "and you must remember that a thing that may sound silly to a man when he's by himself sounds very different when he's with his best girl. You've got to get that moment when a boy wants to squeeze the hand of the girl he's sitting next, and the old married couple simper a bit, and think that after all they've not had such a bad time together.

"And I dare say that is why a play like *Romance* seems so bad to the critic. He's gone there by himself, when he should have gone there with a girl. *Romance* has got all the sure hits; it's steeped in amber light. All the effects, the hidden singer, the one passion, the woman that never marries. But you must not go to a show like that by yourself."

What others have done unconsciously, Milton Hayes has done consciously. He knows exactly what he is doing, and in consequence relies less on chance than others of his profession, and if, as he promises, he takes to writing musical comedies after the war, there should be very little doubt of his success.

The week at Karlsruhe passed very quickly, and very pleasantly, and I was thoroughly sorry to have to leave, especially as Tarrant and Stone were on the permanent Red Cross staff. The prospect of a new camp at Mainz offered hardly any attractions. There would be nothing there; no library, no sports outfits; we should have all the trouble of starting the machinery of a "lager." Not one of us looked forward to it.

CHAPTER IV

THE HUNGRY DAYS

§ 1

THE entrance of the Citadel Mainz was calculated to inspire the most profound gloom. An enormous gate swung open, revealing a black and cavernous passage. As soon as all were herded in, the gate shut behind us, and we were immersed in darkness. Then another gate at the end of the passage creaked back on unoiled hinges, and ushered us into our new home. That cobwebbed passage was like the neutral space between two worlds. It laid emphasis on captivity.

Under the lens of the mendacious camera the entourage of the citadel presents a very pleasant aspect. The square looks bright and large, the rooms light and airy; from the top windows there is a delightful view of the Mainz steeples and of the Rhineland hills, and a fleeting glimpse can be caught of Heine's bridge. But to the jaundiced eye of the *Gefangener* all this comeliness was illusion. In actual circumference the square measured about 400 yards, and it was too full of the ghosts of squad drill. On most of the walls were painted the head and shoulders of dummy targets, that a regiment of snipers had once used for rifle practice. The spirit of militarism was strong; and however delightful the Rhine may look when photographed from the top-story window of a tall block, it is less arcadian when viewed through a screen of wire netting. The whole place was littered with sentries, and barbed wire. For not one moment could one imagine one was free. At times even a sort of claustrophobia would envelop one. The desire to move was imperative, and the tall avenue of chestnuts seemed to rise furiously, as though they were sentinels that would some day draw all things to themselves.

Some of the rooms were, it is true, light and sunny. But the rooms in Block III were miserably dark. The windows were on a level with the ground on account of a moat that ran round the building, and in front a line of chestnuts shut out the sunlight. The rooms were long and narrow, with bars across the windows. At the end it was very often too dark to read; the window sill was the only place that provided enough light for a morning shave. From the outside and from the inside the block was like a dungeon, and the official photographs omitted to immortalise it.

The routine of the camp was very simple. At eight o'clock in the morning breakfast, consisting of coffee, was brought to the rooms. At half-past nine there was a roll-call. At twelve midday there was lunch in the mess-rooms; at three in the afternoon coffee was brought round to the rooms; at six there was supper in the mess-rooms. At nine the doors of the block were closed; at nine-thirty there was an evening roll-call; at eleven lights went out.

OUR DAILY ROLL.
[To face page 48.

But for two fortunate contingencies those early days would have been almost unendurable. One of them was the arrival from Karlsruhe of Tarrant and Stone. During our first week every evening brought a draft of new arrivals; and among one of the later of these appeared Tarrant and Stone, staggering beneath the accumulated kit of fourteen months' imprisonment. The change contented them little. After the shelter and privacy of a room for two, it was no joke to be dumped into the publicity of a room of ten. The creature comforts were missing. Naturally we showered sympathy. But as a practical philosophy altruism is a sadly broken reed. The pleasure at the prospect of their company quite outweighed the inconvenience that its presence had caused to them; and, besides that, they brought with them no small part of a library. The bookless days were over now. No more should I have to spend a whole morning over the only volume in the room—The Book of Common Prayer. No more should I have to go to the most extreme lengths of subservience to borrow *Freckles* or *The Rosary*.

The other piece of luck we had was in the weather. During the early days of May the square was bathed in a metallic heat; and as soon as roll-call was over a deck chair was pushed into the shade of a tree, where one could doze and read throughout the whole morning, and forget that one was hungry.

For those were hungry days. Indeed it is hard not to make the first two months a mere chronicle of sauerkraut. I honestly believe that the Germans gave us as much food as they could, considering we were "useless mouths": but it was precious little. After all it is one thing to be reduced to short rations by slow gradations, but it is a very different thing to be taken from the flesh-pots of France where one eats a great deal too much, to a vegetable diet that was not nearly sufficient. There was only one proper meal a day: lunch. We then got two plates of soup, three or four potatoes, and a spoonful or two of beetroot or cabbage. The effect lasted for three hours. Supper rarely provided potatoes; usually two plates of thin soup, and sauerkraut or barley porridge. In addition there was a fortnightly issue of sugar, a weekly issue of jam, and a bi-weekly issue of bread. On this last issue the *Gefangener's* fate depended. Life simplified itself into an attempt to spread out a small loaf of bread over four days. It did not often succeed. On the first day one carefully marked out on the crust the limit at which each day's plunderings must stop. The loaf was divided, first of all, into four equal parts, then each quarter was again marked out in divisions; so much for breakfast, so much for tea, so much for supper. It did not work. Each day removed its neighbour's landmark. By the third day only a little edge of crust remained. It was demolished by tea-time, and nothing quite equalled the depression of the evening of that third day. The worst time was at eight o'clock. The effect of a slender supper had by then worn off, and there was the comforting reflection that for sixteen hours there was not the least likelihood of being able to lay hand on any food; and the dizziness of a breakfastless morning is an experience no one would wish to indulge in twice.

They were strange days, and strange things happened. Money ceased to have any value unless it could be turned into edible substance. Those with big appetites carried on a sort of secret service to obtain bread; fabulous sums were offered for a quarter of a loaf of bread that contained less flour than potatoes; and, at a time when a mark was worth a shilling, there were those who were prepared to pay seventy-five marks for a loaf; and twenty marks for half a loaf was the lowest rate of exchange.

One knew then the emotions of the man with threepence in his pocket; who is feeling ravenously hungry and knows that, if he spends that threepence on dinner, he will have nothing left for the next day. It is an alternative that in terms of brown bread has presented itself to every prisoner of war.

The psychology of semi-starvation would make an interesting study; and it would bring out very clearly the irrefutable truth that the only way to get any peace for the mind is by throwing sops to the physical appetites; that passions must be allayed, not suppressed; and that the moment anything is suppressed it becomes an obsession. For there is poison in every unacted desire, and the only way to deal with the appetites is to be neither their slave nor tyrant. Asceticism renders a clear view of life impossible.

And during those days, if one sufficiently objectified one's emotions, there would be always found the insidious germ working its way into the most unlikely places. Even in books there was no escape from it; it deliberately perverted the author's meaning. And one occasion comes back very vividly. I was reading *La Débâcle* and had reached the scene where Louis Napoleon is sitting alone in his room, and his servants lay before him dish after dish which he leaves untouched. And because of this perpetual hungriness the whole effect of the incident was spoilt. I could not get into the mood necessary to appreciate the effect Zola had aimed at. All I could think was, "Here is this appalling ass Louis Napoleon, surrounded with meats and fish, entrées and omelettes, and the fool does not eat them. If only they had given me a chance!"

It was interesting, too, to notice its effect on a man like Milton Hayes. Naturally it hit him in that most vulnerable point, his theory of Popular Taste.

One morning I found him sitting on a seat, dipping into three books in turn, *Lorna Doone*, *Pickwick Papers*, and *The Knave of Diamonds*.

"A strange selection," I said.

"No," he said; "they are all the same, really. They've all done the same thing; they've sold; they've got the same bedrock principle somewhere, and I think I've found it."

"Well, what is it?"

"Gratification of appetite. All these accounts of big meals and luxury. That's what gets over. People don't want psychology. But they'll smack their lips over the dresses and feasts in *The Knave of Diamonds*; and then look at the venison pasties in *Lorna Doone*, and the heavy dinners in *Pickwick*.

That's what people want. They have not got these things; but they want to be told they exist somewhere, and that they are there to be found. If ever you want to write a book that will really sell, remember that: gratification of appetite: make their mouths water."

<h1 style="text-align:center">§ 2</h1>

There was, of course, in the form of the *Kantine* an official method of supplementing the ordinary issue. And across that counter strange things passed.

Every day provided a fresh experiment. A rumour would fly round the camp that there was a new sort of tinned paste to be had, "I saw a fellow coming out with a biggish-looking tin," some one would say. "I don't know what was in it. But it was too big for boot polish."

There would follow a general rush, and a queue thirty deep would prolong itself outside the door. The mixture would turn out to be a green paste purported to be made from snails and liver. For a day or two the unfortunates who had bought it spread it over their bread, and tried to make themselves believe they liked it. The only purpose it really served was to make the bread look thicker than it was.

Then another tin would appear; there would be another rumour, another rush to the door, another disillusionment. There was a crab paste, a vegetable paste, a nondescript brown paste; all in turn went their way, and yielded to the soft intrigue of Dried Veg.

Dried Veg presented itself very innocuously in a paper bag covered with directions in German. It looked dry and unappetising. None of us knew how it should be treated,

THE "KANTINE" AT MAINZ.
[To face page 56.

but the consensus of opinion decided that half an hour's boiling was all that was needed; and so adhering to the popular idea, we emptied the packet into a saucepan full of water, boiled it for half an hour, and ate it. It was really not so bad.

Within half an hour, however, we knew that something was wrong. All of us began to move uncomfortably. Pain spread itself across our stomachs: and then too late appeared one who could translate the instructions on the wrapper. The contents should have been left to stand in water for at least twenty-four hours, by which time it would have absorbed all the moisture demanded by its composition. We had given it only half an hour's boiling. It took its revenge by swelling silently within us.

It was a terrible night.

From these expenditures it will follow that life at Mainz was not quite so cheap as might be imagined. And we were unfortunate in being captured at a time when the value of a mark was very high. For, thanks to the business instincts of our German bankers, a cheque for three pounds was worth only sixty marks.

Myself I do not pretend to understand bimetallism, rate of exchange, or any of the other commercial problems that regulate the value of money. But the equivalent of the sixty marks paid monthly by Messrs. Cox to the German Government appeared in our pass-books at that time as £2 10s. 6d.; and as at our end we had to pay £3 for the same number of marks, one is driven to assume that the intermediary German firm was making a profit of about sixteen per cent. on every cheque drawn; a basis on which we would all like to run a bank.

The result both of the rushes to the *Kantine* and the succeeding rushes to the Paymaster's office was the distinguishing feature of our daily routine—Queues. For the first impression of a stranger entering the citadel would have been of a sequence of trailing lines receding from open doors. Every department had its own particular queue. There was the queue outside the library, an insignificant affair owing to the thinly lined shelves; the queue outside the tin store for those who had parcels, and the two main streams of humanity, the queue from the *Kantine*, and the queue from the Paymaster's office. These two last were in a continual state of flux, a ceaseless ebb and flow; the moment that they seemed likely to be engulfed within the welcoming portals there would be another meeting of the ways, more applicants would arrive, and the human rivers would overflow their banks. To any one who enjoyed this pastime, life was prodigal of entertainment. He could flit from one dissipation to another. But to the majority it was a tedious business, and the art of "queuing" began.

For an art it certainly was. As the master of finance is always watching the rise and fall of the markets, so that he shall know the exact moment at which to buy or to sell; so the master queuist would bide, waiting for that moment when the stream would be at its lowest ebb, and when he might safely attach himself to its interests. The cowardly might enrol themselves stolidly at an early hour, and shifting forward slowly, almost imperceptibly, they would eventually reach the doors. For them there was in queuing neither colour nor excitement. It was a dead level.

But for the artist in queues it was altogether different. He hazarded much. He had to work out whether or not it would really pay him to get to the door of the *Kantine* an hour before it was due to open. If he waited till later on in the day, he might manage to take advantage of some quiet lull, and gain his ends after a paltry thirty minutes' wait. But, if he did, there was always the chance that when he did arrive the article he had desired would be no longer there. The whole stock of liver paste might have been exhausted. An appalling contingency. All these considerations had to be weighed.

And with regard to the Paymaster's office there were attached notable risks. At noon every day the gates were closed, and consequently at about half-past eleven the applicants ceased to arrive. Nobody cares to wait thirty minutes and then have the doors shut upon him; and it was here that the genius of the queuist was most in evidence.

At half-past eleven he would look at the queue: there were fifteen people waiting: would those fifteen people be able to draw their cheques in time? and in cases like this a mere average of time was valueless. In queuing, as everywhere else, all standards were relative. Because on one day twenty people had drawn their money in as many minutes, it did not follow that on another fifteen would draw theirs in an hour. Nationalities had to be taken into consideration. Those twenty men were probably Irishmen. But if there were ten kilts outside the gate, even when the hands of the clock stood only at a quarter-past eleven, the great queuist would turn away. He knew that to each of those ten Scotsmen the Paymaster would have to explain the theory of exchange in indifferent English, which would not be understood, and that the Paymaster would then have to try and gather the drift of a Scotsman's logic in a language he had not heard before, and that for each individual applicant an interpreter would have to be summoned.

Queuing, if refined to an art, required a great deal more than the merely neutral quality of patience.

THE QUEUE OUTSIDE THE PAYMASTER'S OFFICE.
[To face page 62.

CHAPTER V

THE PITT LEAGUE

§ 1

AT the beginning of May we had all resigned ourselves to a stay of at least two years in Germany. After that we should be probably exchanged, or interned in a neutral country. Perhaps the war might be over. At any rate soldiering was more or less done with; and the eye began to turn once again towards civilian occupations. In consequence the Future Career Society was born.

It opened very modestly, under the auspices of a field officer and two subalterns. Its programme was to find out what each person wanted to learn, and to provide classes as far as was possible in the required subjects. It was hoped to bring together members of the same profession and form circles for Schoolmasters, Bankers, and Farmers.

This scheme presented countless opportunities for the Bureaucrat. There is in every community a certain number of people who are never so happy as when they are confronted with a host of particulars that demand tabulation. They glory in the sight of a ledger, ruled off into meticulously exact columns. They love to write at the top of each column: size of boots, colour of hair, number of distinguishing marks.

To such a one was entrusted the clerkship of the Future Career Society. It was announced that at such and such an hour he would receive applicants. Wishing to learn French, I attached myself to a queue, and after a wait of twenty minutes duly presented myself at the desk.

I was received with the stern official gaze that seems to say, "Now then, young fellow, I'm a hard-worked man and can't afford to waste time on you. Let's get to business at once."

"Name?"—Waugh.

"Initials?"—A. R.

"Married?"—No.

"Single?"—Yes.

"Children?"—None.

"Age?"—Nearly twenty.

The questions followed each other with the rapidity of machine-gun bullets. These preliminaries over, he looked up at me with the benevolent

Fairy Godfather expression of, "Now, young fellow, I'm doing my best, I want to help you, but you must meet me half-way."

"Now," he said kindly, "what work did you do before the war?"

"None at all," I answered truthfully; "I was at school."

"Then you don't know what you are going to do when you get back?"

"Oh, something to do with books," I hazarded.

"Ah, yes, Book-keeping. Then I suppose that what you want is a really sound commercial education?"

And he was about to jot down "Commerce" when I pointed out that what I really wanted to do was not to keep books, but to write them.

"Journalism? Then why couldn't you say so at once," and he returned to the official "Busyman" attitude.

Finally we reached the stage to which this examination had led.

"Now, then, what classes do you think of taking up?"

"French."

He looked at me, doubtfully avuncular.

"You know, I don't know whether French will be much use to you. Is that all you are taking up? Because, of course, French is very amusing, but from a commercial point of view really I should advise shorthand. No? well, then, I must just put you down for French. Some notices will come round about the classes."

And he began his inquisition of my successor. Really, considering that to be entered in a French class was the whole object of my visit, the interview was sufficiently prolix, but the fellow enjoyed doing it. That was the great thing.

Like all innovations, the F.C.S. (as it appeared on official abbreviations) met with great support, numerous classes were formed, so numerous, in fact, were they that there was hardly enough room for them. At all periods of the day students could be observed hurrying across the court, a stool under one arm, and a pile of books under the other. The whole day was mapped out into periods; there was no vacant spot but it had to serve as a classroom; and the attendance was admirable. Over a hundred officers attended the first lecture of the shorthand expert. The elementary French class was so large that it had to be divided up into three.

Great trade flourished then in the *Kantine*. Otto's Grammars were at a premium. They were hoarded deliberately. One enterprising linguist went so far as to amass within the space of a week, grammars of Spanish, French, German, Italian, Arabic and Hindustani, together with their keys.

It did not last long: within a week the numbers were diminished by a half; they then sank to a quarter, then an eighth. Within a month no class numbered more than half a dozen, which was just as well, for really people do not want to be taught things. Educational experts who spend years working out theories do not make a sufficient point of this. It is not enough to form a system, and expect the world to fit into it. Only a very few desire knowledge, and those few should be catered for. They will profit by instruction. But those who are taught things against their will, speedily forget whatever they have learnt. There are, it is true, those men who can inspire a love of work, who can produce results from any material, but they are not schoolmasters. There is rarely more than one in each school. For the profession presents insufficient attractions to the really brilliant man, with the result that schoolmasters are drawn from the ranks of mediocrity; and as long as this state of things continues, all that the average schoolmaster can hope to do is to keep the lazy in order, and impart his knowledge to those who want to learn. For the masses education can only mean information, and information by itself has little value.

And so within a month the educational life of the camp had assumed modest limits; but, as those who remained were genuinely keen, the classes became infinitely more efficacious. Conversational French, for instance, was possible as it would never have been in a gathering of thirty. For the enthusiasts the decreased numbers were in every way advantageous, but it gave no pleasure to Colonel Westcott.

Colonel Westcott was one of those delightful persons whom captivity had turned into a burlesque. He was as extravagant as a character out of Dickens, and it was hard to believe in his reality. He was so exactly the type of army officer that is caricatured on the music-hall stage. He had all the foibles and loyalties of his caste. He believed fearlessly in discipline, in the Anglo-Saxon race, in an Utopia made not with hands but with muskets.

In the time when his enthusiasms had been kept in control by the business of war, he had been an excellent soldier; but once captured, he had no outlet for his temperament. Looking down on the court from the window of his room, he was horrified at the thought of so many subalterns passing out of his hands, out of the hands of discipline back into the individual energies of civilian life. And Colonel Westcott hated individualism: he liked to see humanity moving forward in one compact body, with himself at its head. He loathed, and was frightened by, the small bodies that went their own way and in their own time. During the four years of war nothing had given him more pleasure than to watch the slow conscription of England. In it he saw unity and safety. He was with the majority and was therefore safe.

But now all those good things were ending. He saw the splitting up of all this common impulse into countless cliques, with interests not his own; and he felt that he must make one effort before the close. For Colonel Westcott was a brave man. He would sell everything for the comfort and assuagement of his soul. And so he founded the Pitt League.

As an essay in the floating of a bogus company, it was a notable achievement. Never was such a web of words woven round such a dummy. Not that the Colonel spake one word that he did not believe. He was impeccably honest. He really valued the goods that he extolled.

One evening in the theatre he laid his wares before us. With an unconscious skill, he began by an appeal to the vanity and the emotions of his hearers.

"Gentlemen," he said, "I have been told by one of the padres that in the lesson for March 21st, the day on which most of us were captured, occurs the text, 'Be thou a ruler even in the midst among thine enemies.' That, gentlemen, is what I want to say to you to-night. Be rulers, I will tell you how."

The prospect of gaining the mastery over the generous supply of armed sentries was alluring. There was an instant and unanimous attention.

"We can only do it in one way, gentlemen, and that is by combination. We must all work together, we must work not towards individual prosperity, but towards the prosperity of the community. No longer can we fight our enemies in the field, but we can wage a silent war, we can prepare ourselves so that afterwards we may be triumphant. We must work collectively: we must unite: the life of this camp should be like one machine, in which you are all cogs. And so, gentlemen, I have brought forward my scheme. I have called it the Pitt League, because, well, gentlemen, because it rhymes with *grit*."

And then followed an exposition worthy of the great Tartarin. But even the hero of Tarascon can hardly have brought to play in the account of his visionary Saharas such a fancy, such an overwhelming unreason, such a complete contempt for the bounds of probability. Slowly idea followed on idea, slowly the colossal fabric was raised. That Colonel Westcott was a caricature must always be kept in mind; but even so I think the excitement of the moment must have caught him up. Even he could not in cold blood have conceived such fabulous creations.

The scheme began by amalgamating The Future Career Society; and starting at the point where that society had wisely halted, proceeded to include every department of Imperial life. Committees would be formed; debates and lectures arranged. A research committee would be able to provide information on any subject; a trade and commerce department would provide a comprehensive study of the growth of trade and of Colonial expansion. It would work out every problem of navigation, and every fine question of markets, their rise and fall. A department for home affairs would provide recipes by which thirty million people could live without competition. Divorce, Politics, Education, State control of vice, small holdings, all these would be settled. And then the Dominions, each Colony would have its own department, where Colonials would decide on how best they could further the Imperial ideals. Then there was the regular soldier side, the Imperial Force branch. And here perhaps the Colonel's fancy flew farthest and highest, military strategy would be dealt with from primeval time. Sand-maps on the floor would show the site of battle-fields and the dispositions of the rival armies; tactics would be exhaustively discussed. A new and infallible method of attack would be evolved for the next war.

And all these activities would be accomplished, in spite of the fact that no one in the camp possessed the least information on any of these points; and that as a remedy for their defect there existed neither a reference library nor the likelihood of obtaining one. But by this Colonel Westcott was nothing daunted. Perhaps at the back of his mind there was the unconscious knowledge that the end is nothing, the means all, "and that to move is somewhat although the goal be far."

"And when we go back to England," he concluded, "you will be able to effect the reforms you have thought out here. You will go back with a collective and not an individual patriotism. You will be capable of really efficient citizenship. We shall still be able to move forward as one body. That is the Pitt League, gentlemen."

And then followed the sentence for which he deserves immortality.

"It's my scheme and I like it. I know you'll like it too."

He had out-tartarined Tartarin. Caricature in one human frame could go no further.

§ 2

The Pitt League fared as might have been expected. It was born and christened amid much enthusiasm. The whole camp found itself enrolled under some branch or other, elaborate programmes were devised. The walls of the theatre were covered with notices. Every Wednesday the heads of each branch met in what was called the Parliament of the Pitt League, of which Colonel Westcott was Prime Minister. This gave the required semblance of unity and collective patriotism. A few field officers and senior captains found that a certain amount of work had devolved upon their shoulders, but the life of the average subaltern continued undisturbed. In practice no one is a collectivist, unless it is likely to prove to his advantage. No one wants to be a cog in any machine that does not produce tangible results; and though the camp gave the Pitt League its sympathy and encouragement, it did not see its way to further any interests not its own. The Colonel, however, was quite content with his work. He was Prime Minister of his own Parliament, and everywhere his eyes were confronted with tabulated evidence of his enterprise.

"A very different camp," he would say to himself. "There is now a purpose and an end ... a thorough change of attitude, and," he would proudly add, "it is all my doing."

From this energy, however, there did spring two incidental results: one touched me personally, the other only in as far as I was a member of the general community. The former was that I discovered my name on the syllabus of the Home Affairs branch as a future lecturer on Social Reform, a privilege which was deferred weekly with considerable ingenuity until the signing of the Armistice absolved me from my promise; the other was the inauguration of the Priority Pass.

For it is one of the traits in human nature that no sooner does a man begin to do any work for which he is not paid than he demands recognition of some sort. He wants to be differentiated from the rest. The man who has served twelve months as an A.S.C. batman clamours for an extra chevron. Why should he be ranked on the same level as the infantryman who has only been in the line thirteen weeks. The officer who censored letters at the Base in the first October of the war demands a riband to show he is not one of those mere conscripts who only landed in 1915. They are working of course not "for glory or for honour." Their service is perfectly disinterested, all they want is to be of help to the nation. But still, they do think, that in common justice some sort of difference should be made, some privilege perhaps....

And it was so with the officials of the Pitt League. They all maintained that it was their greatest delight to be of service to the camp, that they were collectivists of the truest and most practical kind. Yet they were only human, and when they saw lazy officers reaping where they had themselves sown, the wedge of justice slipped itself beneath the barrier of their altruism. The elemental idea of "mine and thine" once firmly planted, strengthened and took root. They felt the need of recompense.

For some time they were in doubt as to the dress in which public gratitude should be arrayed. But at last the shorthand expert was gifted with an inspiration. Triumphantly he bore his commodity to the premier.

"Sir, couldn't we have precedence in queues?"

"Precedence, Wilkins?"

"Yes, Sir, we have such a lot to do, that really we have not time to waste half the morning in queues. Couldn't we have a pass or something so that we could go straight in?"

"Oh, yes, admirable, Wilkins, admirable. A Priority Pass, the very thing."

And so the abuse of privilege began.

The camp, not realising what it would lead to, received this news with equanimity.

"Quite right too," was the general opinion. "These fellows do a lot of work. They have not got too much spare time."

Within a day or two the opinion changed. For holders of passes always used them at the same time, that is, when it was most inconvenient to the rest of the queue. For the chief joy of a privilege lies in the flaunting of it before the eyes of the less fortunate. There were low murmurs of resentment.

Two afternoons later I met Stone in the last stage of exasperation. After a stream of abuse, the "sad accidents of his tragedy" became clear.

It was a wet, windy afternoon, and Stone had been waiting in the "cheque" queue for over an hour. He was heartily sick of it, but had been particularly anxious to draw his money before roll-call, having booked the billiard-table for immediately afterwards. And it had really looked as though he would be just in time. Five more minutes, and he was fourth in the queue; a minute a man. It should have worked out all right.

Slowly the queue had moved forwards. Too slowly for Stone. There had been a delay of almost two minutes, because some ass had not been able to remember the amount of his cheque. Numerous sheets had to be turned over. It was "a bit thick."

But at last the three men in front of him had been disposed of. With a minute to spare, he had just been about to walk into the office, when a voice had bawled, "Half a minute," and a diminutive captain had rushed up panting.

"Just in time."

"Afraid you won't get in before roll-call," Stone had said, sunning himself in his serenity.

"Oh, that's all right. I've got a Priority Pass."

"A what?"

"A Priority Pass."

"But what for?"

"Botany. Ah, there's that fellow coming out. My turn, cheerioh."

And thirty seconds later the bell had gone for roll-call.

"It's the limit," said Stone, "the absolute limit, and do you know what that absurd botany ass does, two hours a week, that's all. Damn it all, and then he can just saunter into a queue whenever he likes. I've a jolly good mind to get a Priority Pass myself, it's quite easy, all you've got to do is to invent a language that no one else is likely to know. Finnish, say, and old Westcott would be only too bucked to have another branch to his 'Up dogs and at 'em' League."

To invent a language.

The idea ran through my mind, a glimmering thread of thought. What was it George Moore had said? A new tongue was needed. The day of the English language was over. It had passed through so many hands, been filtered in so many places, that it was now colourless and without significance. But this new tongue, this child that was waiting to be cradled; it was a lyre from which any rhythm might be struck; it was virgin soil that would bear epic upon epic, masterpiece on masterpiece; and it would be so simple, so childishly simple. All that was needed was the purchase of an Otto-Sauer conversation grammar which we could translate into Finnish. No one would be any the wiser. Colonel Westcott could be taken in quite easily.

I began to picture the scene.

Stone and I would go to him one evening, when there had been potatoes for supper. We should find him well filled and satisfied, puffing contentedly at a cigar, and musing sentimentally over an ideal world peopled with the Anglo-Saxon race, bred on collectivism and eugenics.

He would greet us with a kindly patronising smile.

"Well, Stone. Yes, and let me see, who is it, Waugh. Well?"

"Well, Sir, the fact is that Stone and myself have been thinking a good deal lately about our duties as citizens. We were wondering whether we were really doing all we could. It's such a splendid opportunity here, Sir. We could lay the foundations of so much."

"Certainly, Waugh, certainly, an admirable thought."

"And, Sir, we were wondering whether you had ever considered the possibilities of Finland, Sir."

"Finland, Waugh."

"Yes, Sir. I believe it's the coming centre of the herring trade, and I'm sure if some of these fellows here realised it, they would be only too keen to try their luck there, and it would be a great thing for the Empire, Sir, if we could collar the herring trade."

And Colonel Westcott, whose ideals of citizenship were more surely laid than his knowledge of commerce, would not be able to withhold a grunt of assent.

"But, Sir," I should go on, "the fact is that in order to trade with the Finns one must be able to speak their language, and you see, Sir, it's the only language they've got, and they're very sensitive about it."

"Of course, of course, very natural, very natural indeed."

"And, Sir, Stone and I, well, I've lived there a good deal, and so has Stone, and we thought, Sir, it might be a good thing to start a Finnish class."

"Admirable, Waugh, of course, if you think you can do it."

"Oh, yes, I think we could, Sir," I should explain. "As I said to Stone, 'we owe a duty to the State as well as to ourselves, and it would be very selfish if we went to Finland alone.' It's our duty as citizens, Sir, to think, not in terms of the individual, but of the community."

Almost an echo of the Colonel's own sentiments as expressed in his most recent jeremiad. How benignly he would beam on us, how he would recognise in us the objectification of his ideal.

"I'm very glad, very gratified indeed that you should feel like that," he would have said. "It's the right spirit, the sooner you start the class the better."

We should have risen to go, but at the door we should have turned back.

"I'm sorry to trouble you again, Sir," I should say, "but there is just one little point. It'll mean a great deal of work for Stone and myself. We shall have no grammar or anything."

"Of course, Waugh, I can quite see that."

"And there's very little spare time with these queues and things."

"Oh, but I think we shall be able to manage that," Colonel Westcott would say. "I don't see why you shouldn't both be given Priority Passes. It's a very unselfish work, I'll see about it. I think it'll be all right."

And within two days our names would appear on the already lengthening list of privileged persons.

And then what would happen? The Finnish class would follow the course of all our studies in the Offiziergefangenenlager, Mainz. Upwards of thirty would attend the initial lecture. Within a week this number would have sunken within the teens, from which it would gradually recede to the comfortable proportions of five or six. For these few enthusiasts we should cater, and for their righteousness, as aforetime for Gomorrah's, would be issued the divine dispensation—a yellow ticket.

And what a language it would be. With what fancy would the common articulation of the everyday world be passed into an æsthetic mould. How arbitrary would be the rules of taste, what a harmonious blending of sibilants and liquids. How George Moore would glory in our creation.

And then I supposed we should begin to tire of our toy; the novelty would wear off; the lyric impulse would be lost. It would degenerate into hackwork. And then we should try to get rid of it; with a sort of false sentimentality we should muse over the pleasant hours we had spent with it, and wonder if the affection had been returned, almost as the hero of a French novel sighs over a discarded mistress.

Then, of course, there would be Colonel Westcott. We should not wish to disillusion him, to show ourselves as we really were. We should wish to maintain the deception to its end. His opinion of us would be very high.

We should present ourselves to him apologetically, as men for whom the burden of reforming mankind had grown too heavy. We should give the Colonel the impression that he and we were pioneers in advance of our age, stationed at the outposts of progress; that where we stood to-day, the world would stand to-morrow. But in the meantime....

"You see, Sir," I should say, "there are only four fellows learning Finnish, and none of them, if I may say so, seem to me the sort of fellows we really want. They're more of the class of chap who learns a language merely to be able to say he knows it, and really, Sir, I don't know if it's worth our while to spend so much time on them. You were talking the other day about conservation of energy, Sir."

The Colonel would bend confidingly. So far this catchword had not suggested itself to him. But it was surely only a matter of time.

"And," I should continue, "we thought we'd be really doing better if we were to learn a language ourselves. Stone thought the same, Sir, but he said, 'We must ask Colonel Westcott first.'"

"Ah, quite right, quite right, it's no use wasting our forces. If fellows won't back you up, well, it's their fault, not yours. You've done your best."

And doubtless in that moment the Colonel's thoughts would be flying forward tentatively to the grey days of demobilisation, to the sundering of the one river into its many streams. And he could see himself standing there at the parting of the ways, his averted eyes turned back to the pleasant pastures, to the unity and harmony of war. He could see himself as the last relic of a more golden era, of a cleaner if not more clever world.

"And you really think, Sir, that we have done our best?"

"No doubt about that, oh, none at all," he would sigh. "I only wish we had a few more like you in the camp. It's the right spirit."

And we should acknowledge the panegyric with a smile, and leave him to his dreams and aspirations, his Pan-Saxon Utopia.

But it could not be done. In actuality the scheme would lose its glamour, its wayward charm. It was better to let it remain in the imagination, the fresh counterpart of some less noble phenomenon. *Aimez ce que jamais on ne verra pas deux fois.*

CHAPTER VI

THE GERMAN ATTITUDE

DURING those early days the chief interest of our life lay in the insight it gave into the conditions and psychology of the German people. For nearly four years we had been at war with this nation, and yet we knew practically nothing about it. For four years an iron screen had been drawn between us and them. All the information that we received came to us through the filtering places of many censorships. We were told only what the authorities wished us to be told; and of the countless activities of Germany, report reached us of none that could bring credit to any nation but our own. But now we were able to converse freely with German officers and soldiers, and form our own opinion as to their attitude towards us.

Of course this opinion is subject to numberless qualifications. Even from the highest window of the citadel only a limited view can be obtained of a country that has been the subject of so much calumny and conjecture. Our impressions were confined to one province and one town in that province; they cannot be said to represent the mentality of Germany as a whole; and of the five hundred officers confined within the barracks, each individual has brought home with him a different idea of Germany and the Germans.

And again, it may be that personally I have been rather fortunate in my experiences. Baden-Hessen is one of the least Prussianised Provinces in Germany, and officer prisoners of war are treated a great deal better than the men. But I do believe that the conversations I had with various Germans, both soldiers and civilians, give a fairly accurate index to the attitude of a large number of the enemy.

What came as the greatest surprise to me personally was the absence, to a considerable extent, of all vindictiveness and hate. Evidence goes to prove that there was in the early months of the war a good deal of collective hate; and as a relic of this there were in the shops picture postcards of sinking battleships headed "Gott strafe England," and the cartoons in the illustrated papers such as *Simplicissimus* and the *Lustige Blätter* were all to the tune of "my baton drips with blood." But the *Frankfurter Zeitung*, which is the representative paper of that part of the country, was absolutely free from articles headed "The English Beast" or "The Devilish Briton." It afforded an ideal example of journalistic continence.

And it was the same with their poetry and literature. There was much verse inspired by the same violence as "The Hymn of Hate." There were numberless sonnets starting off, "England, du perfides land," and it is only this sort of stuff that we have been allowed to read in England. This is the standard by which the Germans have been judged, and it presents them in a very false light. For after all, if the "hate" verse that is scattered throughout the English Press were to be taken as representative of the ideals and the aspirations of the race, we should show up none too well. For with the majority, no sooner does a man try to put his thoughts into words, than he loses his bearings. He does not write what he feels, but what he thinks he should feel. All that is genuine in him is inarticulate, and the obvious rises to the surface. And it has followed that in the last four years there has been an incredible quantity of bad verse written and very little good. But that little good is the key to the English temperament. The secret longings of the individual have been revealed not in the type of poem that goes—

"We mean to thrash these Prussian Pups,
We'll bag their ships, we'll smash old Krupps,
We loathe them all, the dirty swine,
We'll drown the whole lot in the Rhine."

They have found their expression in the deep and sincere emotion of such poems as "Not Dead," by Robert Graves, J. C. Squire's "The Bulldog," Robert Nichols's "Fulfilment," and Siegfried Sassoon's "In the Pink."

And working from this basis, it is surely more just to judge Germany less by the cheap vehemence of Lissauer than by those quiet poems that, hidden away among pages of opprobrium and rhetoric, enshrine far more truthfully those emotions that have lingered in the heart of the suffering individual from the very beginning of time.

There is a poem on a captured trench that opens with a brief word-picture of the scene, the squalor, the battered parapet, the dead men. "Over this trench," the poet continues—

"Over this trench will soon be shed a mother's tears.
Pain is pain always,
And courage is true wheresoever it may be found.
And in the hearts of our enemy were both these things....
That we must not forget;
Germany must love even with the sword that kills."

That sentiment is universal, it contains the complete tragedy of conquest.

And indeed for the individual soldier war is the same under whatever standard he may fight. German militarism may have been the aggressive factor, but the individual did not know it. Unless a people feels its cause to be just, it will not enter into the lists. If it is the aggressor, then that people must be hoodwinked. The victory lust of 1914 was a collective emotion springing from the German temperament and from their belief that they were in the right. The individual soldier went to battle with feelings not too far removed from our own.

"The war was a crusade to us then," a German professor said to me; "we felt that France and Russia had been steadily preparing war for years. We felt that they were only awaiting an opportunity. The Russians mobilised long before we did. They drove us to it."

It was in that spirit, he told me, that the German volunteer armed himself in August 1914.

"But of course," he said, "it didn't last long. The glamour went soon enough. And now, well, all we want is that the war should cease."

And in the spring of 1918 the individual outlook in many ways resembled that of France and England. There was the same talk of profiteers, of the men who dreaded the cessation of hostilities, of the ministers who were clinging to office. There was the old talk of those who had not suffered in the war. It was all very well for the rich, they could buy butter, they did not have to starve. They managed to find soft jobs behind the lines. They did not want the war to stop. Indeed, the resentment against the "shirkers" and "profiteers" was more acute than the hatred of the Allies. For after all, emotions like love and hate are not collective. One can only hate the thing one knows.

And from conversations with this German professor emerged the spiritual odyssey of his nation. The change from enthusiasm came apparently very quickly; probably because the Alliance suffered so heavily in loss of life, and because its internal troubles were so great. The war weariness had not taken long to settle; for many months peace had seemed the only desirable end, and victory in the field was regarded as important only in as far as it appeared the safest road to this goal. Victory *qua* victory they no longer desired.

This the Imperialists and pan-Germans must have realised, and they had made it their business to persuade their people that without victory peace was impossible. A significant illustration of this is afforded by the change of catchword, as displayed on public notices. Below some of the early photographs of the Crown Prince was printed "Durch Kampf zum Sieg"—"Through battle to victory," and this represented the early attitude;

but by the time that we had arrived in Germany this had been changed. On many of the match-boxes was a picture of a soldier and a munition worker shaking hands, and beneath was written, "Durch Arbeit zum Sieg: Durch Sieg zum Frieden."

This was what the Imperialists had to keep before the people if they wished to retain their office and their ambitions. The people were no longer prepared to sacrifice themselves for some abstract conception of glory and honour. They wanted peace, and as long as their armies were able to conquer in the field they were prepared to believe that that was the way to peace. But if their hopes proved unfounded, they were in a state of readiness to seek what they wanted by other means.

It was no longer "zum Sieg" but "durch Sieg"; and in view of what has since happened, I think, this is an important thing to grasp.

CHAPTER VII

PARCELS

§ 1

TOWARDS the middle of June parcels began to arrive, and the camp became a very whispering gallery of rumours. It started with a wire from the Red Cross at Copenhagen stating that a consignment of relief parcels had been dispatched. From that moment, there was no incident of the day that was not somehow construed into a veiled reference to Danish bread.

Lieut. Jones would meet Lieut. Brown on the way to the library.

"Any news this morning, Brown?"

"Nothing official."

"Then what's the latest rumour?"

"Well, I shouldn't put too much trust in it, old man," Brown would answer guardedly, "but I saw Colonel Croft talking to one of the Unter-officers this morning."

"Did you hear what they were saying?"

"No," said Lieut. Brown. "You see, I can't speak German, but by the way they were gesticulating and all that, I feel pretty certain it was about these parcels."

And within two hours it was common knowledge throughout the camp that the Unter-officer of Block II had told Colonel Croft that there were two hundred parcels within the camp.

As the days passed, and no consignment arrived, conjecture exceeded every bound of possibility. It was asserted on the one hand that the parcels had been commandeered on the way by the German army, and on another that the parcels had actually arrived and were in the camp, but that the Commandant had refused to issue them till he had received instructions from Berlin. During these days there was no epithet with which the word Boche went uncoupled.

At last, however, the parcels did arrive; a large cart was perceived entering the gate laden with cardboard boxes, and a roseate mist enveloped the outlook of the *Gefangener*. The lean years were at an end, prosperity was in sight, and the flesh-pots of Egypt already steamed within the imagination. "Bread's in the citadel, all's well with the world."

But one thing had been overlooked. A composition of milk and flour is not improved by the delays of a protracted journey through the metallic heats of a German summer. The bread was unbelievably mouldy.

Well, we tried to imagine that we enjoyed it, and it was certainly something to eat; we doctored it and applied every remedy that the ingenuity of the R.A.M.C. could devise; but there are limits beyond which redemption cannot pass. There are stains which only dissolution can annul, and the freshness of white bread once lost is as irrecoverable as virginity. Green it was, and green it remained. The taste of mould was there and baking would not remove it.

Perhaps there was some comfort in the assurances of the doctor that, after it had been soaked and heated, it could do no active harm: but it could not change the nature of the object. Sadly it was agreed that bread was a washout.

However, it served a moral if not a physical purpose. It was the prophet of the sunrise, the false dawn that was the inevitable herald of a readjusted life. If bread could come from Copenhagen, it followed that the grocery parcels from London were not so immeasurably remote.

For weeks they had appeared on the horizon far withdrawn, invested with Utopian glamour. Orderlies who had been captured since Mons had told us what tins each parcel of the cycle would contain. The list of delicacies had been devoured by eager eyes, but their existence had always savoured of the impossible. They were the dreams of some incurable romantic; there could not really be such things, at least not in Germany. But now they actually began to approach within mortal gaze; after all, the Citadel Mainz was not so utterly separated from the rational world. The authorities in England had apparently realised that some six hundred officers were beleaguered there upon those ultimate islands. An agreeable reflection; and, once more, conversation centred wholly upon food.

And a more barren topic could hardly be discovered. Perhaps some romance might be woven round the intricacies of a Trimalchio's banquet, and a distinguished novelist made one of his characters woo triumphantly his beloved with a dazzling succession of French *pâtisseries*; but bully beef and pork and beans are too solid a matter for anything but a moral discourse. They have no lyric fervour, their very sound is redolent of platitudes, and from the beginning of the day up to the very end to hear nothing but panegyrics on their composition,—it was indeed a trial.

A "PRISON CELL."
[To face page 104.

§ 2

It was not till the end of June that parcels began to arrive at fixed and regular intervals, and those were days of great excitement. Each morning at 8.30 a.m. the names went up on the notice board, and immediately a cry ran round the barracks, "List up." Pandemonium broke loose. The laziest *Gefangener* leapt from his bed, pulled on a pair of trousers, dived into the safety of a trench coat, and rushed for the board. In that space were waged Homeric contests. Some hundred brawny soldiers were all struggling towards a small board, on which fluttered the almost illegible carbon copies of the sacred list. There was much craning of necks, and driving of elbows, much cursing and much apologising. The weak were driven to the wall; and even when a forward surge had borne the eager aspirant to the portals of his inquiry, there remained for him the ardours of retreat. Through a solid square of humanity he had to drive his harassed frame.

These were moments of high excitement and of an equivalent depression. Those to whom the rush for the board had seemed too hazardous an exploit waited impatiently within the room for the tidings of some enterprising herald. Anxiously they would lean out of the window looking for a returning comrade.

"By Jove," some one would say, "look, here's Evans coming."

"Has he signalled anything?"

"No, but he's coming awful slow. There can't be anything for him."

And sadly Evans would re-enter the room from which he had set forth with such gay hopes.

"One for you, Turner; and you've clicked, Smith, two for you; and Piggett, you've got one. Nothing for the rest."

"Nothing?" echoed the rest.

"No," Evans would grunt, and for him, as for the other unfortunates, the remainder of the day had lost all savour and romance.

For the lucky, however, the excitement of the morning had only just begun, and a mere name on the parcel list served but as a preliminary excitant. The real zest of dissipation was still in store. Behind the barred doors of the "Ausgabe" lay all the innumerable varieties of an assignation. There might be cigarettes, clothing perhaps, a cycle parcel from Thurloe Place, or, and this was in parenthesis, a mouldy loaf from Copenhagen.

First of all, there was the queue, the inevitable prelude to every form of punishment and amusement; and in this queue conjecture ran wild on the probable percentage of bread parcels in the camp.

"Well, I was standing by the gate yesterday," one fellow was saying, "and I saw a load of parcels come in, and damn me if every one wasn't a Thurloe Place."

"Ah," but the pessimist would break in, "that was the second load, you saw. I watched all three come in, and believe me, in the first and last loads there was nothing but bread."

This, however, no one would believe, and the imparter of this rumour was told to secrete his information elsewhere.

Slowly the queue moved forward, and at last the claimant passed through the sacred portals that were watched over by guardian angels in the form of whiskered sentries with zigzagged bayonets; within the sacred place there were even more seraphim. Behind a long table stood four slovenly civilians, whose duty it was to open the parcels, and see that no sabres or revolvers were concealed beneath the apparent innocence of a tin of Maconochie's beef dripping. At a far corner of the table was the high priest, the master of the ceremonies. He sat there "coldly sublime, intolerably just," with a large book in which he entered every name.

Action proceeded on lines of Teutonic formality. The claimant for a parcel would first of all present himself before the high priest, and murmur the number of his parcel.

"Twenty-one."

This the high priest would translate into German with a commendable rapidity.

"Ein und zwanzig."

He would shout this over his shoulder to one of the many satellites whose work it was to produce the required parcel. The next few seconds would be anxious ones for the hungry *Gefangener*. He would watch the sentry move about among a store of boxes, moving one, displacing another. He would lift a parcel so small that it could assuredly contain nothing but boot polish, and a shiver would pass through the leanly expectant. But at last, after many vacillations and counter-marches, he would emerge triumphantly with a cardboard box bearing the large Red Cross of the Central London Committee.

But even then there was more to be done. Each parcel had to be carefully opened and its contents examined. No tins nor paper could be taken away. Packets of tea and cocoa had to be stripped of their covering and emptied into baskets, while the tinned foods were spirited away to the block cellar, where later in the day they were opened in the presence of a number of sentinels.

The reason for all this palaver we never quite managed to fathom. It was surely enough that the British Red Cross had pledged its word not to include for exportation tracts for the times, pulpit propaganda, or prismatic compasses. With delightful duplicity the German authorities laid the blame of this on to our Allies.

"You see," they said, "we're very sorry, but the French get so many things in their tins; poison for our herbs, and knives and files. We must take precautions. Of course many parcels are quite all right, but the French, you see...."

And to our Allies the Germans told the same tale.

"You see," they said, "your parcels are all right, but the English hide corkscrews in their bully beef. We must take precautions...."

And so another link was added to the immense chain of queues.

At this time, too, letters and books began to arrive, and over these officialdom wound all the intricacies that it could muster. Letters had to be fumigated first, each page had to be carefully censored, and stamped with a large messy blue circle usually deposited over the least legible portion of the correspondence. And every novel had to be read from beginning to end.

Numerous were the regulations. Any reference to Germany was taboo, the mere mention of the word Hun or Boche was the signal for confiscation. Of my first consignment of books, two were suppressed. One of them being rather a prolix novel to the tune of khaki kisses, was not much loss; but the other, Ford Madox Hueffer's volume of poems, I made valiant efforts to save. One evening I caught the censor unprepared, and pointed out to him that the author was a man of complete literary integrity, and that nothing he could write could be looked upon as dangerous.

"Ah, but," the censor expostulated, "it is all full of Huns and Boche."

"Ah, well," I said, "can't you tear those pages out?"

"But then there would be no pages left," and against this assertion argument was impossible. "And you see," he went on, "we are not Huns."

"No?" I said.

"No, the Huns were beaten at Chalons in A.D. 453. You have no right to call us Huns. That is your Northcliffe Press your hate campaign; we are men the same as you."

And it was quite useless to point out that the average soldier applies the nickname "Hun" or "Boche" or "Jerry" in very much the same way as we call the Scotch "Jocks" and the Frenchmen "Froggies."

The censor would not see it. "You think we are all barbarians," he maintained. "It is your hate campaign, and we are not Huns; the Huns were beaten in 453 at Chalons by the Romans."

East of the Rhine there is not much sense of humour.

And indeed, considering the way in which the Kaiser has compared himself to Attila, our warders were peculiarly sensitive on this point. And they always approached it with that strange Teuton seriousness that is for ever hanging over the crags of the ridiculous.

At Karlsruhe, on the preceding Christmas, a certain officer, who had spent most of the afternoon beside a bottle, in the middle of a camp concert arrogated to himself the right to play a leading part. And leaping on the stage, he had for the space of half an hour regaled the audience with an exhilarating exhibition that contained many good-humoured but forceful references to his "sweet friend the enemy." Unfortunately a German censor was present, and the next morning the officer was testily buttonholed by the sleuthhound.

"Captain Arnold," said the censor, "I do not wish to make any trouble between you and us, but you said last night many things that were most offensive."

Captain Arnold, whose memories of the preceding evening were shrouded in a mist of cocktails, endeavoured to be jocular.

"Oh, no, surely not? Not offensive; come now, not offensive."

"Oh, yes, indeed they were; most offensive, Captain Arnold. You called us Huns."

The gallant officer realised that he had been indiscreet, and saw that only one way lay open to him.

"Hun," he said. "But why not, that's what you call yourselves, isn't it?"

The censor looked astonished, and aggrieved.

"But surely, Captain Arnold, you know what is a Hun?"

"Not exactly, no."

"Very good. I will show you."

The next day the censor appeared bearing a history of Germany in three volumes.

"Now, Captain Arnold," he said, "you will find here all there is to know. It is quite simple; no doubt you will be able to borrow a German dictionary, so that you can look up the words. You will find all about it."

For three days Captain Arnold kept the books, and then returned them with many thanks and a promise not to repeat his insults.

"I thought you would understand," said the German censor. "It is only ignorance on your part that makes you call us Huns; and now you will tell your comrades, and they will understand too."

And the little man trotted off, happy in the thought that his race had emerged from the examination triumphantly vindicated.

CHAPTER VIII

OUR GENERAL TREATMENT

A GREAT deal has been said and written on the subject of the treatment of British prisoners of war, and the general idea at the present moment is one of a succession of unparalleled brutalities and insults. That much inhumanity has been shown it is neither possible nor desirable to deny, and it is only just that those responsible should have to give an account of their actions. But it must be borne in mind that though all the instances brought forward are perfectly true and authentic, propaganda aims not at the *vraie vérité*, but at the establishment of an argument; and the individual instances, which have formed the foundations of this conception of inhumanity, do not present a complete picture of captivity, and should not be taken as typical of every prison camp.

Of course one can only write about what one knows. Baden-Hessen is one of the more moderate provinces; and the treatment of officers is infinitely better than that of the men. But, speaking from my own experience, I can say with perfect sincerity that, from the moment when I was captured to the moment of release, I was not subjected to a single insult or a single act of brutality. I was treated with as much courtesy as I should have expected from a battalion orderly-room, and the discomforts and inconveniences of the journey were due in the main to faulty organisation. It sounds bad when one hears that a batch of prisoners were sent on a four days' journey with rations for one day, but the corollary that the accompanying German sentries were provided with exactly the same amount of food casts a very different aspect on the case.

The starvation of prisoners has become almost an axiom, and indeed they were miserably underfed; but so was the entire German people, and the custom of treating prisoners as well as civilians is confined to England. Among all continental nations it is an understood thing that on the scale of diet the enemy should come last, and in Germany there was only enough food for a bare existence.

In this respect, I believe, officers were much more fortunate than their men, and certainly they had the great advantage of a permanent address. For the men were being continually moved from one camp to another. At one time they would be working in the fields, at another in the salt mines, sometimes stopping for a couple of months, sometimes only for a few days. The result of this was that their parcels were trailing after them right across Germany. At times they would go several months without one at all, and then if they had the luck to make somewhere a prolonged sojourn, they might receive thirteen parcels within three days. Of course the men shared out their parcels as far as possible, but they were never certain what was coming next, and they had many very hungry days.

With us there was none of that: we were in a permanent camp, and our parcels when once they had begun to arrive came through regularly. There were delays occasionally, especially when heavy fighting involved congestion of the railways; but eventually we received every parcel dispatched from a central committee. The only ones that did get lost were the home parcels that were sent privately. Everything sent from the Red Cross Committee, or from Harrod's or Selfridge's, arrived intact and in perfect condition.

As regards actual treatment, owing to the fact that officers were not made to work, there were very few occasions when physical violence was possible, cases of this sort generally occurring when men proved intractable in the factories. The only opportunities that were presented were when officers tried to get away, and the sentries availed themselves of these chances pretty generously.

There were four or five attempted escapes, and on two of these occasions the officers were badly mauled by the sentries. The second time that this happened the German orderly officer put a stop to this treatment at once; but on the first occasion the officer stood by while the sentries belaboured their captive with the butts of their rifles.

The would-be Monte Cristos turned to the German officer and asked him if he considered such treatment proper for a British officer.

The German shrugged his shoulders. "Oh, well," he said, "you must expect this sort of thing if you try to escape. You ought to stop in your room."

Before, this particular German had always been especially agreeable to us. The only possible excuse for his behaviour lies in the fact that he was very fond of the bottle, and might have been a little drunk. But however one looks at it, it was a sufficiently discreditable affair.

Of the insults and degradations to which the officers of the camp at Holzminden were subjected we had no experience. The Germans adopted towards us an invariable attitude of respect that was if anything too suave. They were always profuse with promises, but it was very hard to get anything out of them.

"Oh, yes," they would say, "we can do that easily. We will go to the General and it will be all right. Don't worry any more about it. We'll see to it, it will be quite simple."

But nothing ever happened. The simplest request always managed to lose itself somewhere between the block office and the Commandant's study; and gradually we learnt that formal applications were no use whatsoever, and that if any one wished to change from one room to another, the surest way to get there was to collect all his baggage into a heap and move there independently.

The probable cause of this was the General himself, who was one of the most arrogant and pompous little men that militarism could produce. He was the complete Prussian, the Prussian of the music-hall and the Lyceum. Very small and straight, he would strut about the parade-ground clanking his spurs, or else he would stand in a pose, his cloak pulled back to reveal his Iron Cross. And he was utterly vindictive. One does not wish to misjudge any human being, but I feel sure he must have derived an acute pleasure from sitting at his window and looking down on the court, his eyes hungry for some misdemeanour on our parts, in which he might possibly find an excuse for some punishment.

He was certainly given opportunities, and I think that considering the man he was, it would have been judicious to have approached him in a slightly different way. But it always happens that the majority have to suffer for the faults of a few thoughtless people, and several restrictions were placed on the camp that could have been easily avoided. In every community there is the rowdy section, and this rowdiness was accentuated by the lack of freedom. There was no outlet for energy, except a walk round the square, or a very occasional game of hockey. And the spirits of the swashbucklers found expression in "rags" organised on an extensive scale.

But it was unfortunate for those who, having realised that they were prisoners, wished to make the best of their conditions. And really the rags were extraordinarily futile. One sportsman conceived the idea of lowering from the top-story windows dummies which the sentries would mistake for escaping Britishers and fire at. Luckily this scheme was suppressed, but there was nevertheless one night a very large and organised jollification, which was of course exactly what the General wanted.

For three weeks he closed the camp theatre, and put a stop to music and concerts of any description, which meant the removal of the only form of amusement that we had.

On another occasion when bombs were being dropped on Mainz, a few officers began to cheer and shout. It was again playing straight into the General's hands. He immediately stopped for a period of two months all walks outside the camp, and any one who has been a prisoner will know what the curtailing of that privilege meant. It was a great pity, and our prison life would have been much more easy, if only the turbulent few had realised that it was in their own interests to keep quiet, considering the man with whom they had to deal.

Though as a matter of fact I have little doubt that, however well we had behaved, the General would have found some excuse for inflicting reprisals. For he was quite capable of inventing regulations off his own bat. He was a sort of self-elected dictator, and drew up his own code and Army Act. His most scandalous infliction was an order that the covers should be removed from all books before being issued to the camp. The old excuse was brought forward; the French used to hide maps and poison between the cardboard and the cloth.

For this order the General had apparently no authority whatsoever, and it was particularly unjust, because we had been precisely told at Karlsruhe that all books must come direct from a publisher, so as to prevent any danger of their being tampered with. The result was that we had all sent home for new copies of books of which we already had soiled duplicates, and then when the books arrived, we found that they had to be practically cut to pieces.

They told us that the books could be kept for us if we liked, but naturally we did want to read them, now that they had come, and we had no other alternative but to authorise their execution; and surely for the true book-lover there can be no fate more awful than to have to stand in silence and watch book after book being barbarously mutilated.

Occasionally we would try and save a volume. The Bible was the centre of much controversy. There was no reason why it should be regarded as any more innocent than a Swinburne as a possible receptacle for propaganda, but the censor did certainly hesitate over it for a moment. But eventually he did not relent.

"No, I'm afraid it must go," he said; "after all that God has put up with during the last four years, He ought to be able to survive this."

It was the one flash of wit he showed, but it did little to save our covers. To all intents and purposes the books were ruined. The leaves began to turn up at the edges. After a book had been read three times, the glue at the back had cracked, and the pages gradually loosened. It was a sorry business; at least two hundred pounds' worth of books must have been cut up within three months, and there was absolutely no authority for the order. This we discovered later on, when we managed to lodge a complaint before the Central Command at Frankfort. They told us there that they had no objection at all to the issue of books with covers, and the restriction was instantly removed; but in the meantime no small part of a library had been destroyed.

But our chief grievance was a medical one. The organisation of the camp was quite inadequate to meet the demands of any sudden epidemic. In ordinary times it certainly worked well enough. Personally I never went to hospital, but a friend of mine who spent a week in the isolation hospital brought back a very favourable account of his treatment. The food was excellent, and the sister was particularly kind, going out of her way to do everything that lay within her power. But it was very different towards the end of the autumn, when the grippe was raging in the camp to such an extent that in the average room of eleven officers, there was hardly a day when less than four officers were in bed, and the arrangements were very poor. Of course every allowance must be made for the fact that there was hardly any medicine in Germany, and that when a disease had once started there, it was almost impossible to stop it. But the medical attendance was both ignorant and desultory. Those cases that were removed to the hospital were given, it is true, attendance as careful as they would have received in England. But in the camp the doctor appeared to take no interest in his work at all. Very often he only visited the patients once every three days, and when he came he did not take much trouble with them. He used to ask a few casual questions and then say, "Aspirin and tea." The sick had to rely entirely on the other occupants of their room, and the help they received was willing but naturally ignorant. The result was that many officers became very seriously ill, and several of them died. The German organisation was in this case criminally inadequate.

CHAPTER IX

THE DAILY ROUND

§ 1

WITHIN a few weeks, however, the arrival of a parcel had ceased to be an affair of momentous import. We could look on bully beef and Maconochies with comparative unconcern. The contents of each parcel varied only in such incidentals as sugar, chocolate, and packets of whole rice. The framework was the same, a solid enough construction, but one that as a continuous diet proved ineffably tedious. To begin with, we tried to make our meals more interesting with improvised puddings. We mixed a certain number of different ingredients into a bowl of water, beat them up into a paste, and then baked them in a tepid oven. The result was usually stodgy and quite tasteless. Personal vanity prevented us from confessing this, and night after night we struggled through these lukewarm, unpalatable dishes. How long this would have gone on I do not know; when the end came it came very suddenly.

One evening there was a lecture in connection with the Pitt League, and it was rumoured that Colonel Westcott was going to speak. And Colonel Westcott's speeches were such that no one would willingly miss. He had always ready some new panacea, some fresh catchword. As long as he remained passive he was infinitely entertaining.

"We must go to this," said Evans, and with some alarm I noticed that of the five other members of our mess, four were preparing to move seating accommodation.

"That's all very jolly," I said, "but who's going to cook the dinner?"

The answer came back with a startling unanimity.

"You."

"But look here," I began to protest, "you know what I am at these things. I've never cooked a dinner before."

"Time you began then."

And I was left standing before an empty stove. There remained only one other member of our mess, my friend Barron, who spent the greater part of his day asleep. I woke him up.

"Barron," I said, "we've got to cook the dinner."

He blinked up through sleep-laden eyes.

"But, my dear Alec...."

"It's no good," I said sternly. "If we want anything to eat, and I most certainly do, we've got to cook it ourselves."

Slowly Barron rose from his seat.

"Well," he said, "what have you got?"

"There's a tin of bully, some beans, half a Maconochie, we can make a stew of that."

The stew was the work of a second. We mixed it all up with water, scattered some salt on the top, and left it to boil.

"And now the pudding," I said.

This proved a more difficult matter. There was no rice left, and we had used the last of the Turban packets.

"Archie," I said, "we'll have to invent one."

For five minutes we argued about the ingredients. Hodges wanted to give it a fish-flavour by adding a tin of salmon and shrimp paste.

"There's been no taste to the beastly thing for the last six days," he protested. "It might just as well taste of that as nothing."

Finally, however, we decided on what we euphemistically dubbed a chocolate *soufflé*. First of all we spread a handkerchief flat on the table, and sprinkled over it a little cornflour. We then took a packet of cocoa.

"How much shall I upset?" I asked.

We read the directions on the outside, but on the subject of chocolate *soufflés* the manufacturers were sadly reticent. So as there was no clear guide, we used the entire packet.

The mixture now seemed to demand some moisture, so we poured a little warm water on it, and tried to knead it into a dough. But it did not work: a brown paste adhered to our fingers; nothing more.

"It won't bind," said Barron. "We must put some butter with it."

"We've got no butter."

"Oh, well, then, try some beef-dripping."

So the next ingredient was half a tin of dripping, and as regards appearances it certainly had excellent results. A few minutes' hard kneading produced an admirable dough. But when we sucked our fingers afterwards, the flavour was anything but that of chocolate. It had a thick and greasy taste.

"Alec," said Hodges, "this dripping's ruined it."

"Your idea," I said cheerfully.

For a moment he looked fierce, then returned to the matter in hand.

"Something's got to be done," he said; "we've got to swamp that dripping somehow."

"What about some treacle?" I hazarded. "We drew some this afternoon."

And within a minute the bulk of our pudding was further increased by an entire tin of treacle, and whatever its taste after that, it was certainly not of dripping.

"That's about enough, isn't it?" I said.

"Well, you know," said Archie thoughtfully, "I don't really think it would be harmed by some salmon and shrimp. After all, it would help to counterbalance the dripping."

But already I had begun to wrap the handkerchief round the brown sticky ball. When it was firmly incased and knotted, we lowered it into a small saucepan, put it on the oven, and waited for the wanderers' return.

They came back as usual with a great clatter of feet, expressing their hunger in the most forcible terms.

"Hellish hungry," shouted Evans, "and the dinner's bound to be awful if Waugh's cooked it."

"You wait," I said, and plumped the stew down before him. This dish, probably because it had cooked itself, was quite eatable; and there was so much of it that in the earlier days it would have formed a meal of generous proportions. And by the time we had finished it, none of us felt in the mood for any more solid fare. Something delicate and appetising would have been delightful, a *pêche melba* perhaps, but suet ... no. And of course this rather militated against the success of the chocolate *soufflé*.

And to begin with, it was a little burnt. There was a large hole in the encircling handkerchief, and the bottom of the pudding was black. Considering the bulk of the pudding, this had really very little effect; but it prejudiced the others, and the artist has to be so tactful with his public.

And then the pudding itself. Well, if we had not had the stew first, I am sure we should have all enjoyed it; but coming as it did on the top of a heavy dinner, even Barron and myself were hard driven to finish it. And it was only self-respect that made us. The others took a spoonful or two and desisted. Barron and I struggled manfully to the end, and were then conscious of four steely pairs of eyes. Evans, who acted as a sort of mess president, was the first to speak.

"What did you two use to make this pudding?"

"Oh, nothing much," I said, in an offhand way; "a little cocoa, a little treacle, a little cornflour." Somehow I felt I could not confess to the dripping.

"But how much did you use?"

Barron must be a braver man than I am, or it may have been he was still feeling a little sore because the salmon paste had not been included; at any rate he went straight to the point.

"A tin of each."

There was a general consternation. That a whole tin of treacle, half a tin of dripping, a complete packet of cocoa, had all gone to a pudding that only a third of the mess had been able to eat at all ... it was unbelievable, a gross case of misplaced trust, perfidy could go no further.

Barron and myself were not popular that evening. But our peccadilloes bore fruit later. That chocolate *soufflé* served the purpose of a climax. From that day onward it was implicitly understood that no cook should invent recipes for puddings.

§ 2

With the regular arrival of parcels, and the consequent immunity from hunger, our life settled down into that ordered calm which would have been the constant level of our routine as long as the war lasted. And it was here that captivity weighed most heavily.

Before, our routine had always been to a certain extent progressive. We had been a new camp, we had had to form societies and committees. We had a library to build up, and there was always the parcel list to add its daily incentive to enthusiasm. But there came a time, when all these wishes either for books or food were satisfied, and when the individual had to depend for amusement solely on his own resources. Here was the real trial of captivity.

Since my return several people have said to me, "It must have been beastly living among the Huns." But that was an infliction that it required little fortitude to bear. The Huns never worried us, unless we worried them. We could have exactly as much intercourse with them as we wanted, and there was no need to have anything to do with them at all. But there was no escape from the continual presence of five hundred British officers, and the continual conversation of the ten other members of the room. For not one moment was it possible to be alone. And as the evenings grew darker, the doors of the blocks were closed earlier; and by October we found ourselves shut in at six o'clock, with the prospect of a long evening in the room.

Those evenings were simply appalling. We all got on each other's nerves horribly; as individuals we liked each other well enough; but it was no joke to be in the constant company of the same people, to hear the same anecdotes, the same opinions; and, owing to the limited area of common interests, talk always centred on the war. And there is no subject more wearisomely distasteful. By the end of six months' imprisonment nearly every one had got utterly fed up with his room and the inmates of it. Smith would meet Brown outside the *Kantine*, and a conversation of this sort would take place.

"My Lord, Brown, but my room is the absolute limit, it drives me nearly wild."

"But, my dear man, you've got some topping fellows in there, there's Jones and Hawkins and May."

"I dare say, but you try living with them for a bit. You wouldn't talk like that then."

"Oh, well," Brown would say, "you haven't got much to grumble at; if you were in my room, now...."

"But your room, Brown; why, there are some tophole men there...."

And so the world went round. For indeed, however patient one is, it is impossible to live in the same room as ten other men, to eat there and sleep there, to spend half the day in their company, and not get nervy. Before long we had reached that state when we quarrelled over the most trifling things—about the dinner, whether we should have bully beef or a veal loaf. The slightest inconvenience awoke resentment. All the domestic details that cause friction in the married home were with us intensified a hundredfold, because there was with us none of the real and selfless affection which alone can bridge over these difficulties. Things had reached a sorry state by the time we had left; there was hardly a single officer who had a good word to say about his room. What we should have been like after another year I dread to imagine.

As it was, it was bad enough. For myself I never stayed in the room one moment more than I could help. And often in the evenings after the doors had been shut, I used to walk up and down the cold stone corridor with Barron; we would do anything to get away from the room. It was the only way to preserve our balance.

And here in its psychological aspect lies, I think, the true meaning of captivity; for in the bare recital of incidents there must be always a savour of the soulless. The conditions of life are only really important in as far as they form a framework for personality. It is the individual that counts, and the real meaning of eight months' imprisonment does not lie in their political or sociological aspect, but in the effect that they have on character. For each person they had a different message, each person was touched in a different way. Probably through the mind of each individual flitted the same recurring moods, modified and altered by the demands of each particular temperament, but still the moods were the same fingers playing upon different strings.

And for me, at any rate, the mood that recurred most frequently was one of a grey depression, mixed with a profound sense of the futility of human effort. Confinement inspires morbidity very quickly, and some of us used to take an almost savage delight in wrenching down the few frail bulwarks of an ultimate belief. From certain quotations we derived an exultant satisfaction.

"Pleasure of life what is't? the good hours of an ague."

We used to croon the words over to ourselves and endeavour to arrive at some stoic standpoint from which we could completely objectify ourselves and our ambitions.

The wearisome sameness of the days, the monotony of the faces, the unchanged landscape, the intolerable talk about the war, all these tended to produce an effect of complete and utter depression. This was far and away our worst enemy: whole days were drenched in an incurable melancholia. The continual presence of sentries and barbed wire flung before us a perpetual symbol of the intelligence fettered by the values of the phenomenal world. Life resolved itself into a picture of eternal serfdom: sometimes the body was enslaved, sometimes the mind, but there was always some bar to Freedom. It was all so much "heaving at a moveless latch." Purposeless and irrevocable.

It is easy enough to laugh at it all now. But then it was a very real trial. Those doubts and uncertainties, which at some time or another assail all men, and with a great many form a silent background or framework for the events of their mournful odyssey, were with us continually present; and however gloomy a view one may take of the universe, one wishes to be able to escape from it at times. And the only remedy was work.

Indeed confinement must have been a very real ordeal to those whose temperaments were not self-sufficient, and who depended on the outside world for their amusements and distractions. It has been said times without number that the dreamer loses half the pleasure of life, and that he lies bound up by his own fantasies and wayward creations: that he has no eyes for what Pater has called "the continual stir and motion of a comely human life." Well, Pater wrote that of Attic culture, of the light-hearted world that is reflected in the pages of the *Lysis*, and perhaps modern life presents none too comely an aspect. Certainly in place of "stir and motion" we have bustle and excitement, a clumsy fumbling after sensation. Perhaps the dreamer has not lost so very much, and he does at any rate carry his own world with him: he is self-sufficient; within the sure citadel of his own soul he can always find those pleasures which alone have any claim to permanence. Flaubert is always the same, behind barbed wire as in the shadow of a Wessex garden: the change of environment makes no difference there.

But on those who preferred action to contemplation, prison life bore very heavily, and there was something rather pathetic in the various attempts that were made to fight against the growth of listlessness and apathy. To begin with, of course, every one entered his name on the roll of the Future Career Society; no one took less than three classes; there was a general rush to attain knowledge which lasted about three weeks.

After that, life resolved itself for a great many into a laborious effort to kill time, and here the Germans showed their commercial instincts. The *Kantine* authorities catered for this hunger for novelty, and from sure knowledge of the depression of markets gauged the exact moment when each particular craze would begin to ebb.

The first hobby was wood-carving, an affair so hazardous that the first day numbered about ten per cent. casualties. It demanded enormous delicacy. Boxes of all descriptions were on sale, on which were traced patterns of labyrinthic intricacy; one could cut photo frames, cigar boxes, paper cutters, and to accomplish this labour there were provided small knives of a razor-like sharpness, which under the influence of the least overweight of pressure flew off the box at an alarming angle, to bury themselves in the palm of the other hand. It required enormous patience, and to me appeared one of the most monotonous occupations. It took hours of work to complete the smallest job.

This, of course, was not at all what the *Kantine Wallahs* desired. They wanted a hobby which would require a lot of material and very little time. Wood-carving took much too long, and the profits arrived much too slowly, and so they accelerated the slump in wood-carving by the innovation of satin-tasso, which was in every way a far more noble craft.

To begin with, it gave the personality of the artist a fuller freedom. In wood-carving individual preference was hopelessly bound down by the laws of pattern. As in the cast of certain modern painters who having once conceived a "stunt," proceed to pour the most unlikely moods into one artistic mould, the individual was a slave to shapes. Against this, liberty was driven to revolt, and satin-tasso provided the necessary outlet.

Even here, of course, there were, it is true, laws and patterns, but there was full scope for the peculiarities of taste. The satin-tasso box had on it simply the bare outline of a picture. This one cut round with a sharp knife, and then proceeded to colour in with special paints; and in the employment of these paints any extravagance was permitted. Mediæval costumes offered superb opportunities for splendour and pagan gold. Across a pearl-flecked sky emerald clouds could fade into a wash of scarlet. It was truly a noble craft, and the whole business only took a few hours, which was most advantageous both for the suppliers and the supplied.

There is nothing that pleases the craftsman more than the sight of a finished article, and there is nothing that gives more pleasure to the tradesman than the swift return of gigantic profits, and both these wishes were granted. The *Kantine* did a roaring trade in satin-tasso, and the portmanteaus of the artisan grew heavy with trophies and souvenirs.

But all the same it was rather a pathetic sight to see a man of about twenty-eight, in the prime of life, sitting down every afternoon and evening, fiddling about with a piece of wood and a box of paints. He derived no pleasure from it: it merely served the purpose of a narcotic. As long as his hands were employed his brain would go to sleep, and he need no longer see the tedious procession of days that lay before him. He was symbolic in a way of the Public School Education that deliberately starves a boy's intellect for the sake of his body. The type of clean-limbed Britisher, that Public Schools produce, is all very well in its way, and is infinitely preferable to the type produced by any other system, either in England or France. Of that there can be no doubt whatsoever. But the schoolmasters who adopt this line of argument, forget that they are dealing with a material refined upon by the breeding of centuries. The question is not, "Is the material good?" because it is. The question is, "Does Education make the best of this material?" and I am very certain that it does not. Every man should have sufficient part in the intellectual interests of life, to be able to keep his intelligence active for eight months in surroundings that provide no physical outlets. For after all, it is the mind, or, to use Pater's phrase, "the imaginative reason" that counts.

"Thank God that while the nerves decay
And muscles desiccate away,
The brain's the hardiest part of men
And thrives till threescore years and ten."

And it is surely a severe condemnation of any system that its average products can derive no sustenance from the contemplative side of life, that the moment they are out of the theatres, they have absolutely no resources left. It would have given me the most acute satisfaction to have been able to escort there some of the many schoolmasters who so fiercely defended themselves behind the legend, "By our works ye shall judge us," which was exactly what I tried to do.

The narrow limits of our captivity provided us with only one other craze, the last and the most decadent, for which reason, probably, it was the only one to which I succumbed—Manicure. It was really a tempting lure. One evening I went to the *Kantine* to buy a pencil, and saw a row of beautiful plush boxes, in which reposed long-handled files, and scissors, and knives; and beside these were bottles of delicate scents and polishes and powders, strangely reminiscent of Amiens. The lure was too great, and forty marks went west.

From that day onwards our room was a sort of general manicuring saloon. Several of us bought sets, and from 8 p.m. to 10 p.m. we received visitors. As our guests received treatment gratis, and the initial outlay towards the opening of the saloon was sufficiently generous, it might have been thought that our guests came out of the transaction rather well. But they paid richly for their adornment in pain. We were all amateurs, and the manipulation of a pair of curved scissors requires feminine skill; no one has ever yet called me neat-fingered, and those scissors were very sharp. During the operations of our first fortnight, of all those who came to us with gay step, there were few who went away without at least one finger swathed in bandages.

CHAPTER X

HOW WE DID NOT ESCAPE

§ 1

AS military regulations state that it is the duty of every prisoner of war to make immediate and strenuous effort to escape, and as every man is at heart an adventurer, it is not surprising that our languid community was from time to time regaled by the rumours of impending sorties.

No one has ever yet managed to escape from Mainz, and even if the war had lasted for another twenty years, I believe it would have retained its impregnability. For the citadel had been constructed so as to resist the old-fashioned frontal assault, in which infantry without the aid of a barrage endeavoured to demolish vertical walls. Round the buildings ran stone battlements usually fifty feet high. At any point where it would be possible to jump down was stationed a sentry, and between these battlements and the buildings were two distinct chains of wire netting, that were continually patrolled. At an early date I decided that, in my personal case, the possible chances of escape in no way counteracted the enormous inconvenience to which an attempt would inevitably put me. And if I did get away, it would result in the probable loss of the greater part of my library, and of all my MSS. All things considered, it hardly seemed worth while.

But for other and more daring spirits personal inconvenience was a thing of trifling importance. They would talk of their duty, of their hatred of the Hun, of their desire to be in the thick of things again. But the chief allurement was the love of *réclame*: every man is at heart a novelist; and they would picture to themselves the days of "What did you do in the great war, Daddy?" and the proud answer, "I escaped from Mainz," and there was also the glory of standing in the centre of the stage. They liked to be talked about in undertones, to hear a whisper of "Don't tell any one, but that fellow's going to try and beat it to-morrow." They hankered after excitement, and in consequence when their schemes began to ripen to maturity, they enveloped their actions in all the theatrical paraphernalia of Arsène Lupin. It was wonderful what they made themselves believe. Spies were lurking everywhere, and in consequence their every action had to be most carefully concealed. One officer, who thought he was being hoodwinked, disguised himself by shaving off his moustache, and wearing a cap all day to hide the thinness of his hair. Of course to those who really took the business seriously every credit is due. They spent hours preparing maps, and ropes, and many marks in bribing sentries. But to the majority an escape consisted chiefly in a bid not for liberty but for fame. For it was only with the most deep and carefully laid plans that any one could have hoped to get away.

It is unnecessary to say that in the machinery of these enthusiasms our old friend Colonel Westcott played his heroic part. When he amalgamated into his Pitt League such existing organisations as the Future Career Society, he considered that he had taken under his wing all the imperial activities of the camp; and so one branch, and a very select branch, of his scheme included those desirous of freedom. It was quite a harmless affair, this little society, and in no way jeopardised the chances of escape. All that the Colonel wanted was to feel that he had a share in every sphere of the life of which he was the central embodiment. He liked to have these young fellows sitting round him discussing their plans; he liked to be able to drop here and there the necessary words of advice; it was an understood thing that no one was to attempt to escape without first submitting his ideas to the Colonel; and within a brief time this amiable gentleman had led himself to believe that he was the fount from which all these alarums and excursions flowed.

The first attempt did not take place till we had been prisoners a little over four months, but its preliminaries began a good deal earlier. One of the accomplices was in the same room as myself, and for weeks he used to carry about with him an air of mystery. In a far corner of the room he would be observed tracing maps of the various roads to the frontier, and from time to time he would take me quietly aside.

"Don't tell any one," he said, "but I'm going to clear soon, and I'm getting the maps. I tell you, of course, because—oh, well, you're in my room, and all that. But keep it dark."

He spoke like that to nearly all of his acquaintances. It is all very well to talk of breaking laws just for the fun of the thing, but one does want the rest of the world to know what a devil of a fellow one is.

I remember one Sunday afternoon, at school, how I cut the cord of the weight on the chapel organ, with the result that that evening the music suddenly stopped and the choir wrecked. It was a noble piece of work, which I surveyed with a justifiable pride. But I was not really satisfied till I had told the whole house about it; naturally, of course, swearing each individual to secrecy.

"Don't tell a soul, of course, old man. I should get in a hell of a row if it was found out."

Suave, mari magno.... When one is perfectly safe, it is delightful to imagine all the punishments that might have been visited on one, if the Fates had been less kind; we always hunger for sensation; from the security of a warm fire the imagination gloats over the ardours of warfare and the splendours and agonies of adventure. We like to feel that danger overhangs us; we shiver with apprehensive delight beneath the sword of Damocles. We like to be told that there will be a social upheaval within our lifetime. Perhaps it will come in five years' time. Perhaps to-morrow. At any rate, to-day we are secure. And it was in this spirit that the glamorous web was woven round that first escape.

The efforts that were made to avoid suspicion were superb. The conspirators felt that anything might give away their secret. Had not Sergeant Cuff found at one end of a chain of evidence a murderer and at the other a spot of ink on a green baize tablecloth? and so they left nothing to chance. A loose board beneath the stove served as an admirable hiding-place for maps and plans. And in consequence our room was used as a sort of general dump.

It was a great nuisance; they would do the mystery stunt so very thoroughly; and it was such a noisy business. To open their underground cupboard a few nails had to be abstracted, and a few wedges applied. The resultant noise would have woken not the least suspicion in even the most distrustful Teuton, and would have played a very insignificant part amid all the accumulated turmoil of the day. But no risks must be run. And so while the cupboard was being prized open, an operation that would sometimes take over ten minutes, one of us had to be detailed to go outside and break up wood so as to disguise the noise. It was a deafening business, that occurred two or three times each week; and it did not seem as if the contents of this cupboard demanded such strict secrecy. I once asked what they kept there.

"Only a few papers," was the answer, "a compass and provisions for the journey."

That a compass, being contraband, should be carefully concealed, I could well understand. But the papers consisted of a field officer's diary and a few maps abstracted from the backs of a German Grammar; while the bag of provisions contained only those delicacies that we received in parcels, of which chocolate formed the greater part. And a more unhealthy place to store it, it would be hard to find.

"Look here," I said one day, "what's the idea of keeping that chocolate there?"

"To escape with, of course. Splendid stuff for giving staying power."

"But why can't the fellow keep it in his room?"

I was immediately fixed with that sort of look that seems to say, "Good Lord, do such fools really exist!"

"My good man," he said, "how could he keep it there? It would give the whole show away at once. What would you think, if you were a German officer, and found a big store of chocolate in one of the cupboards? What would you think of it?"

There was only one answer to that.

"That the ass didn't like it, I suppose."

But my remonstrance was useless, and soon I began to regard these noises and secrecies as part of the inevitable machinery of prison life.

§ 2

The first attempt savoured, it must be confessed, very strongly of the ludicrous. The protagonists were three colonels who had managed to provide themselves with German money and with suits of civilian clothes, made, so it was reported, out of dishcloths. They chose as their headquarters a room situated directly above the main gate. It was a drop of some forty feet to the ground, and a sentry box was stationed immediately underneath. The chances of getting away were in consequence very small, but there was, at any rate, no need for preliminary manœuvres among the meshes of wire netting. The gallant adventurers relied solely on the somnolence of the sentry. It was a cold, rainy night, and their experience of guards at depôts might well have led them to expect a certain lack of enterprise and enthusiasm on the part of their warder. Nor were they disappointed.

It began to rain heavily, and after a few deprecatory glances at the heavens, the sentry sat down in his box, and within a few moments appeared to be unconscious of the external world. From the window of Block I a rope made out of a blanket was immediately lowered, and the colonel began his precarious descent.

And then the rain stopped.

The sentry, roused apparently by the sudden cessation of sound, blinked, rubbed his eyes, and cast them heavenwards, and saw midway between earth and sky a figure swinging from a rope. Well, he must have been something of a philosopher, that sentry: he was in no way perturbed by the apparition. He rose languidly to his feet, blew his whistle to summon the guard, and waited patiently at the foot of the rope.

It must have been a very amusing spectacle. Very slowly and very gingerly, hand under hand the colonel descended, and when he was within reaching distance the sentry helped him very gently to the ground and escorted him to the guardroom. The other

A GALLANT ATTEMPT TO ESCAPE.
[To face page 162.

conspirators, seeing the fate of their chief, hastened bedwards with all possible speed, and when the orderly officer came round they imitated with considerable ability the righteous indignation of a man who is woken up after a three hours' sleep.

This attempt was the signal for frequent and repeated excursions. The lead once given, there were found many ready to follow it; and there was considerable comfort in the assurance that the sentries had orders not to fire unless they were charged. And so for the remainder of our captivity the camp buzzed with rumours.

No one ever got away. Occasionally the first strand of netting was penetrated, but nothing more; and it must have been a poor form of amusement. For the desperadoes always chose a night of rain and wind in the hope that the sentries might have sought consolation within their huts, and it can have been no fun crawling on one's stomach, over sodden gravel, getting soaked and cold; and as the night of capture was always spent in the guardroom, it was a sport that can have held out few inducements.

For the cowardly, however, it did add a spice and flavour to existence. On these nights of danger we used to lie awake patiently listening. The hours would drift by. Twelve o'clock, one o'clock, it looked as if they had got away after all; and then, sure enough, would come the alarm, two whistles would shriek loud above the drip of the rain, there would be a scurry of feet; and then a few minutes later we would see the unfortunate beings escorted to the cells.... We would do all we could for them; we would clamber on to the window sill and would shout our condolences; and these friendly wishes would on the next day as likely as not serve as an excuse for the General to place upon us some further restriction, as punishment for what he considered an unmannerly exhibition of independence.

Of these bold bids for freedom none stood any very real chance of success, and towards the end they became somewhat discredited, as they involved certain inconveniences on those who had resigned themselves to their fate. There would be additional roll-calls, and precautions. Whole rooms were searched and ransacked, a most disagreeable proceeding. And on one occasion the attempt was made from the theatre, which led to the closing of that hall of pleasure during an entire morning while the complete staging apparatus was overhauled, and examined. This caused genuine annoyance, especially as the ravages of the soldiery delayed for three days a performance that had been the centre of much curiosity and conjecture. And this annoyance became almost indignation, when it transpired that this herald of defiance had provisioned himself for his long journey with nothing more substantial than a tin of skipper sardines, two oxo cubes, and a tin of mustard. The general opinion was that if a man was "such a damned fool as to carry that sort of stuff about with him, he had no right to try to escape, upsetting arrangements and all."

And on this type of sally the theatre incident rang down the curtain. But under this category it is impossible to number the attempts of Colonel Wright. His methods were very different; they were not showy; he did not talk about what he was going to do. And as a result he very nearly succeeded.

The chief ingenuity of the Scarlet Pimpernel lay, as far as I can remember, in his grasp of the fact that it is the obvious that evades suspicion. Sentries are on the lookout for an escape by night, but by day they are off their guard. And working on this plan, both Colonel Wright's attempts were made by daylight. Indeed they were both so simple that in cold blood they looked quite ridiculous. The first attempt failed completely, and but for his later achievement, one might have been tempted to wonder how the gallant colonel could have expected any different result.

Alone of the Pitt Escape League he literally did not progress a yard; not one foot did he advance. In broad daylight he was arrested where he stood, or rather, where he sat, for it was in that position that he was discovered.

The plan was not elaborate. Once a week a cart from the laundry came to collect dirty linen from the camp and take it away to be cleaned. And to keep a check on the returns, a British orderly always went with it. Colonel Wright's scheme was to impersonate the orderly, to get himself conducted safely outside the gates, and once there to rely on his own speed and ingenuity to effect an escape. It might have come off; there was an outside chance, remote certainly, but still a chance; however, he was given no opportunity of gauging his share of the two requisite abilities. It is true he got into the cart and sat quietly in a far corner; but before even the harness had begun to jingle, he had been recognised and arrested. A grey business, but he was in no wise daunted. And within a few weeks he had his hand to the wheel again.

His second scheme was considerably more elaborate, but was none the less sufficiently obvious. Zero hour was fixed for half-past five, and at five o'clock in a far corner of the square preparations were begun for a boxing match. Towels and chairs were set out, sponges and bowls of water appeared, and two brawny Scotsmen shivered in greatcoats. There had been no previous notice of this engagement, but interest was speedily kindled, and within a quarter of an hour quite a large crowd had assembled. The close of the opening round was the signal for a marked display of enthusiasm. And it was in the middle of the second round that Colonel Wright made his dash. No one noticed him. The sentries were absorbed in the boxing, and those whose attentions showed signs of wandering were engaged in conversation by two field officers who could speak German. And Colonel Wright, clad in a suit of civilian clothes, cut through the wire netting of the first entanglement, and dashed across the open. In a few seconds he had swarmed over the second series and was out of sight. It was a most daring and brilliant piece of work. All that remained for him now was to lie till nightfall in the shadow of the wall. Then when it was dark he could choose an auspicious moment and lower himself to the ground.

It was a plan that certainly deserved success, and as the hours passed we began to hope that some one had at last got clean away. There was some anxiety lest his absence should be spotted at roll-call, but when nine o'clock came and went, we felt that all was well. And then just before ten o'clock the two whistle blasts rang out. Colonel Wright had been retaken.

And if the story that we heard afterwards is true, chance was outrageously unkind. He had waited till it was quite dark, and had carefully watched for the moment when the beat of the outside sentry carried his warders out of earshot. He had then lowered himself from the wall; and it was here that his luck deserted him. For a couple of lovers had selected that particular part of the battlements as a shelter for their amorous dalliance. And the point at which Colonel Wright would have landed was removed from them by scarcely a dozen yards. He was instantly detected. Yet, with a very little luck, things might still have turned out favourably; for the man, who seemed sufficiently intrigued with his partner, gave him only a cursory glance and returned to the matter in hand; but the woman, with an eye to advertisement, characteristic of her sex, gave expression to her feelings in a series of piercing shrieks. Colonel Wright was instantly arrested.

The sentries found on him a hundred marks of German money, and a railway ticket to Frankfurt. And if he could only have got clear of the camp, I believe he would have had little difficulty in getting to the frontier. For he spoke German excellently and had friends in that part of the country. He had also the nerve and ingenuity which alone could have rendered such a feat possible. This the authorities must have realised; for a few days later he was moved to another camp. What he did there, we do not know. But rumour has it that on the journey he made three more attempts to break away. And doubtless in a camp with fewer natural defences he would sooner or later have succeeded in outwitting his captors.

But as regards Mainz the gloomy record of its impregnability still stands. At one time or another it has been the temporary home of Russians, French and English; all three have in their turn tried to escape, and all have failed. After four years of warfare Mainz is still the inviolable citadel.

CHAPTER XI

THE ALCOVE

EACH week the Pitt League posted up on the walls of the theatre a notice of the times and places of the various classes that were to be held. There were some six rooms at the disposal of this enterprising society. There was the attic at the top of Block I, a noisy room because the dramatic society would probably be found rehearsing next door; then there was the theatre, an impossible room; in the first place because it was too big, and in the second because the scenic artists behind the curtain carried on a continual dialogue to the tune of: "Where is that blue paint?" "Have you put up the wings?" "Where the hell's the hammer?" which dialogue the scene-shifters accompanied with suitable crashes and landslides. It was a poor room for study—the

THE BILLIARD ROOM AT MAINZ.
[To face page 172.

theatre; and then there was the field officers' dining-room—that was not too bad. But one window-pane was missing, and there was no heating apparatus, and the orderlies were always wanting to lay the plates; altogether there was not a superfluity of spare space; there was really only one decent room—the Alcove—and that was for one hour of the day allotted to the botanists and anatomists. For the rest of the time an agenda at the bottom of the Pitt League poster announced that "the Alcove was reserved for authors, architects and other students."

The Alcove was a small room opening out of the billiard-room, and its possession by the "authors, architects and other students" was a privilege jealously guarded. Not that we ever resorted to force, the mere strength of personality was sufficient. A few acid epigrams drove the intruders away with the impression that after all there were lunatics in the camp. Only one man stayed for more than an hour, and that was Captain Frobisher, a large, fat man who was doubtless an excellent soldier, but who was not an addition to a literary society that prided itself upon its exclusiveness. After all, when one is searching for a lost rhyme, or trying to make an honest scene sufficiently obscure to protect Canon Lyttelton's delicate susceptibilities, it is disconcerting to have to listen to a conversation of this sort:—

" ... And what do you think of the new offensive, Skipper?"

"Oh, we'll wipe the swine off the face of the earth. I hope our men don't take too many prisoners. There's only one sort of Hun that's any use, and that's a dead one. Excreta, that's all they are, excreta.... What I say is, smash 'em, and then when they're down tread on 'em. That's all they're fit for. A good Hun is a dead Hun."

Of course such rhetoric is excellent in its place, and in the mouth of a politician would appear as the supreme unction shed over the warring banners of humanity. But there are times....

Frobisher must go. We all decided that. The only difficulty was that ... well, even in confinement one must show respect to a senior officer. It would have to be done with considerable tact; we could hardly approach him ourselves. We supposed that if he really wanted, he could defend himself on the ground that he was a student, a student of the philosophical interpretation of a dozen cocktails. But yet he had to go. And finally Stone undertook the job.

It took two bottles of Rhine wine to screw him up to the proper pitch, but we got him there at last; and nobly did he fulfil our trust. It was an unforgettable afternoon. Captain Frobisher was sitting at the middle table discussing over a bottle of wine his schemes for the entire destruction of the German race. The old saws were rolling smoothly from his tongue.

"We must let them have it; what I say is, starve them out, bomb their towns, confiscate their colonies; then make them pay right up to the hilt, a crushing indemnity. They'd have done the same to us. An eye for an eye. That's the principle we must work on, a tooth for a tooth." Even a patriotic bishop could not have been more humanely vindictive.

And then we led in Stone.

He sat on the edge of the table nearest to the captain; his huge head of hair was flung back in a wild profusion, his shirt was open at the throat, he looked for all the world like a second Byron. And for the space of an hour he lectured on the higher life. As a testimony to the potency of the Rhine vintage, it was without parallel. It was a noble exposition.

He began with Schopenhauer; the jargon of metaphysics reeled into anacolutha: the absolute, the negation of the will; the thing in itself; phenomena, and the real. The mind was dazed with the conflicting theories of causation, and after each sounding peroration he recited in a crooning monotone the less cheerful musings of the Shropshire Lad; while we, entering into his mood, gazed up at him with enraptured eyes, murmuring: "Delightful! Oh, delightful!"

Captain Frobisher fidgeted nervously on his form, he moved first to one extremity, then to another. Periodically he attempted a conversation with his companion; but every time he began, Stone broke into a state of fervour more than usually impassioned, and Frobisher's attention was irresistibly drawn towards this strange creature who had emerged suddenly out of a world he did not know. Stone realised his traditional conception of the romantic poet, the long-haired, sprawling, effervescent creature that he had never seen, but that he had been told the war had killed. And here into the very centre of Mainz, into this home of militarism, was introduced the loathsome atmosphere of Paris and the Café Royal, this unpleasant reincarnation of the hectic nineties.

For an hour he stood it, and then Stone arrived at the point to which all his previous eloquence had led. "I don't know," he said, "I have thought it out for a long time, but I am still uncertain as to which of all the collective emotions has done most harm, has wrought most damage to the suffering individual. Once I thought it was religion, religion with its bigotry and ritual, its confessional and chains; but during the last four years I have been sorely tempted—sorely tempted, my dear Waugh—to believe that of all the evils that can befall a community, there is none worse than the scourge of Patriotism."

It was the limit, beyond which even the endurance of a soldier could not pass. Captain Frobisher threw at Stone one glance charged with distrust, and strode from the room. He never entered it again; and the "authors, architects and other students" were able to return to earth, and become once more respectable citizens.

Of the architects and other students we saw very little. Occasionally a linguist would drift in with a conversation grammar and a notebook, and sometimes a financier would draw up tables of expenditure and loss, but on the whole the Alcove was the property of "Wordsmiths."

There were about five of us in all, and as soon as *appel* was over we used to proceed towards the billiard-room laden with pens and paper. At this early hour there were usually not more than three of us, as Tarrant and Stone preferred to take breakfast at a later hour; but Milton Hayes was invariably to be found there, embellishing lyrics, or putting the final touches to his musical comedy, and in the intervals of production expounding his latest æsthetic theories.

A vivid contrast was presented by Tarrant and Stone. With popular taste they were both equally unconcerned. Relative merit interested them not at all; their standards were deep-laid and inelastic.

Tarrant usually appeared in the Alcove at about one o'clock, and observed a ritual that would with any one else have savoured of affectation, but was with him perfectly natural. Nature had endowed him with generous proportions, more built for comfort than for speed; and he accentuated the natural roll of his gait by his strange footwear. A pair of field boots had been abbreviated into shoes by the camp cobbler in such a way as to admit of the insertion of two fingers between the leather and the instep. To keep them on his feet as he walked, Tarrant had to resort to a straddle that was one of the features of camp life. And as he entered he bulked largely in the door of the Alcove, marvellously shod, carrying under one arm a dictionary, a notebook and a Thesaurus, and over the other a cardigan waistcoat and a green velvet scarf.

He flung his books noisily on the table and then proceeded to array himself for the ardours of composition. He first of all divested himself of his collar and tie, and wrapped round his throat the green velvet scarf, that would have lain more appropriately as a stole on the shoulders of an ecclesiastic than it did as a muffler on those of a *Gefangener*, engaged on a psychological study of seduction. Tarrant then removed his tunic, disclosing a woollen waistcoat, over which he proceeded to draw the second woollen coat that he had brought with him. He explained that they brought him physical ease.

"You see, old man," he said, "it's not much use my mind being free, if my limbs are encased in even the loosest of military tunics."

He then proceeded to work.

Every writer, of course, has his own particular foible, and Tarrant's was an appalling accuracy in gauging the exact number of words that he had written. Most writers are quite content to add up the number of lines in a page, then find the average number of words in a line and multiply. But Tarrant would have none of these slipshod methods.

"On that principle," he said, "I suppose you'd call a line a line whether it goes right across the page or not?"

"Yes," I confessed.

He gave a grunt of contempt.

"And then you say *The Loom of Youth* is 110,000 words long; why, half the lines you call ten words long only consist of two words—'Bloody Hell.' That's not the way to do things."

And so Tarrant laboriously added up every word. It became quite a mania with him. So much so, in fact, that he used to embark on long discussions as to the derivation of amalgamated words, and whether "lunch-time" should count as two or one. For his rough draft he kept beside him a small slip of paper, on which at the end of each sentence he used to make mathematical calculations, that reminded me of school cricket, the scoring box, and the attempt to keep level with the tens.

Correction involved much labour. At the end of the sentence he might have noted down 277 words. Then he would revise; half a clause consisting of eight words would be omitted, and on the slip of paper down went 269. Then a celibate noun called for an adjectival mate, and 270 was hoisted amid applause. It was an amusing game, but it took up a great deal of time. Very rarely did Tarrant produce more than 400 words as the result of three hours' work, and his absolute maximum for a day was 1100.

"All great men work slowly," he said. "Flaubert took seven years over *Madame Bovary*, and I shall take only a year over this," and with a sudden sweep he flashed the discussion back on to his pet subject of words.

"You see, I've done 48,374 words, and there are three more chapters of approximately 3000 words each. Now will that be enough?"

I told him that Mr. Grant Richards had stipulated in one of his weekly advertisements, that if he liked a book, it could range between the limits of 45,000 and 200,000 words, and Tarrant once more returned peacefully to his addition.

Stone, Tarrant's constant companion through the tedium of eighteen months' imprisonment, was chiefly conspicuous for his conversation. Nobody ever actually saw him writing, or had indeed read anything he had written, but he always carried about with him a notebook, that gave the impression that he had either just risen from his labours, or was merely waiting the inspiration of the moment. As a scholar and a critic he was easily the most brilliant of our little circle, and it was delightful to hear him dethrone the idols of the twentieth century. He had very little use for any critic since Pater, or any novelist since Sterne. Of the modern novelists he maintained that the only two worth considering were H. H. Richardson and Arnold Bennett, though to Gilbert Cannan he extended a hand of deprecatory welcome. Wells was the chief target of his wit.

"I don't know what to make of him," he used to say. "Sometimes I think we may almost excuse him on the ground that if he had not written the *New Machiavelli*, *Perkins and Mankind* would not exist. But, really, as I read his recent stuff, *Marriage*, *The Soul of a Bishop*, *Joan and Peter*, why, Max has ceased to be the parodist of Wells, Wells has become the parodist of Max."

As an actual "Wordsmith" Stone enjoyed a reputation something similar to that of Theodore Watts. One felt that he had only to publish what he had written, and he would receive world-wide recognition. In the notebook that never left him, he was supposed to carry the key that should unlock his heart. There lay two completed poems, and a tenth of a novel. But they were quite illegible. None of us ever saw them. Occasionally when the influence of Rhine wine had somewhat weakened the phenomenal barrier that separated Stone's mentality from the real world of his metaphysics, he would promise to inscribe them for us in the morning in the full indelibility of purple pencil. Once he even went so far as to recite one of them; but the words came to us droningly sweet through a mist of inaudibility, and there remains only the recollection of certain sounding words, a low murmur as of a distant waterfall. In the morning all the promises were forgotten, and sometimes I have been tempted to wonder whether those poems had any real existence in the sphere of phenomena. Stone was so at the mercy of his metaphysics, he indulged in expeditions into a world whither I had neither the wish nor the ability to follow him, and perhaps he merely imagined those two poems as some manifestation of that inexplicable "Thing-in-itself" over which he was so concerned. Perhaps they had no counterpart in that draggled notebook; and though it is quite possible that some day we shall see those poems immortally enshrined in vellum, personally I rather doubt it.

Those hours in the Alcove contain all I personally would wish to remember of my captivity. It was a delightful room, with its white tables and windows opening on the fowl-run; it was a perfect place in which to write. The click of billiard balls, and the murmurous rise and fall of inaudible conversations provided the ideal setting for thought. Personally I can never write in a room that is quite silent; its isolation frightens me, and through an open window I listen in vain for the indistinct noises of humanity.

And then towards evening, when the labours of the day were ended, we would sit together round a bottle of a villainous brand of *Laubenheimer* and discuss the merits of Tchecov and de Maupassant. Long contests were waged there on the vexed problems of æsthetics; the limits of dramatic art, *vers libre*, the function of criticism. All these in their turn passed through the sieve of dialectic. At times even captivity seemed a pleasant business, so full of leisure was it, after the bustle of the months that had preceded it. And no doubt years hence, when the rough outlines have become gently blurred against a harmonious background, we shall cast a glamour over those lazy days, and see in them a realisation of Bohemian dreams, of a Paris café and Verlaine leaning over a white table-cloth declaiming his lovely valedictory lines. And perhaps Time, that great alchemist, may even go so far as to transmute that foul white wine into the purest absinthe. We shall think of Dowson and the Cheshire Cheese, of the Rhymers' Club and the delightful artifice of the nineties, and we shall claim companionship with those brave innovators to whom a finished work of art was a sufficient recompense for their weariness. But within it was not really like that; and as Pater has said, no doubt that ideal period of artistic endeavour has never had any existence outside the imagination of the dreamer, sick with a sort of far-away nostalgia, a vague longing for wider prospects and less narrowing horizons. Every generation has flung its eyes backwards over the past, and thought "if it had only been then that we had lived—then, when the values of life were still clear and simple," and round certain names and ages there has been woven in consequence the thin gossamer of Romance, and the artist has found comfort in his conception of a world that has been passed by. From these backward glances and averted faces has emerged much that will never pass—Thais and Salambo, Henry Esmond and Marius the Epicurean.

During the last three years I have often wished that I had been born thirty years earlier, at a time when the influence of French literature was making itself so keenly felt, and when Verlaine was the light about the young men's feet. It is a glamorous world that we catch glimpses of through the opening doors of Mr. George Moore's confessions. But I suppose that really it would not have been so very wonderful after all, and that those delicate creatures whose feet moved through Symons's verse to a continual rustle of silk and cambric, were probably the most tawdry of *grisettes*, and those Paris cafés and the many-coloured glasses of liqueur, they were very much like the Alcove, I expect; and the Alcove is a place where no one would wish to sojourn indefinitely.

But we shall always look back at it with some affection. We spent there many happy hours, and there the weariness of captivity was relieved by the human comradeship that alone makes life endurable. We shall not easily forget how, when the billiard-room was closed for the night, we used to step out into the square, just as the sunset was flooding it with an amber haze, and walk beneath the chestnuts, prolonging the conversations of the afternoon, until the cracked bell and waking lights drove us back to the barracks. I shall never forget those evenings. Probably never before was the citadel—that home of militarism—the scene of so much artistic discussion; and it may be that in after days our ghosts will linger round those memorial places, and that on some quiet evening two tenuous and ungainly forms will be seen swinging down the avenue beneath the chestnuts—

"Dans le vieux parc solitaire et glacée,"

and the sentries of some Jäger regiment will catch the sound of thin voices floating across the night. They will be still arguing over the same old questions, those two foolish ghosts, those questions whose solution the rest of the world has long since decided to ignore.

"But look here now, honestly, surely Brooke is not too bad; listen to this ..." and the faint words of "Mamua" would be borne over last year's leaves.

But the elder ghost would shake his head; and a thin reedy voice would pipe—

"No, it won't do, old man, won't do, only a whispering gallery." And they would pass on, still arguing, still differing, and still, apparently, very good friends.

And the two German sentries would look at one another sympathetically.

"Kriegs-gefangeners, Fritz," one would say, "captured in the great war. There were a lot of 'em here, and those two, you'll always see them walkin' up and down there talking the most awful rot, all about poetry and things. Poor fellows! probably a little wrong in the head, they were, a bit maddish you know; they look a bit that way."

And it is not for me to deny it.

CHAPTER XII

HOW WE AMUSED OURSELVES

§ 1

IN only one province did Colonel Westcott, our genial factotum, place a voluntary check upon his own activities. His sphere, he decided, was confined within the elastic boundaries of education, moral conduct and Pan-Saxon philosophy. And he accepted these limitations with the quiet resignation of one who owns three-quarters of the globe, and deems the remainder to be a land of frost and snow. In other hands he laid the responsibilities of the sports and entertainments committees. And for this reason, perhaps, they were the two most productive bodies.

For the average *Gefangener*, however, games were hard to get. Germany is not athletic in the sense that we are. Militarism has made muscular development the supreme good of all outdoor exercises, and in consequence the authorities thought they had sufficiently catered for our physical propensities by the erection of a horizontal bar, and the largess of some iron weights. Well, that is hardly our idea of sport; and as a nation I do not think we shall ever show much enthusiasm for Swedish drill, P.T., trapezes, and the various devices of a gymnasium, that leave so little room for individuality. The allegiance to a green field and a leather ball, small or big as the season demands, will not be shaken. And at Mainz there were neither green fields nor leather balls.

The gravel square was the only open space we had, and it was uncommonly hard to fall on. There was one football in the camp, belonging to an orderly, that was from time to time the centre of an exhilarating display. But it was a dangerous pastime; every game resulted in at least three injuries, and a scraped elbow was no joke in a country

OUR PRISON SQUARE.
[To face page 194.

devoid of medicine. Only the very daring played, and soon most of them were "crocked."

For a month hockey enjoyed an ephemeral popularity, and a league was arranged, in which nearly every room entered a side. While they lasted those games were great fun, and they were capital exercise. But before very long all the sticks had been smashed, and all efforts to replace them were unavailing, and though a few individuals who had had sticks sent out from England were able to get an occasional game, for the great mass of us hockey ceased almost as soon as it had begun.

The only other game was tennis. As there is no rubber in Germany, this had to be delayed till the late summer, by which time balls and racquets had arrived from England. But what is one court among six hundred? Only a very limited section of the camp could play, and those whose abilities were slight did not feel themselves justified in engaging the court to the exclusion of their more able brethren. And the whole business really amounted to this: that although a newcomer to the camp would see the square at nearly all moments of the day occupied by some game or other, for the average *Gefangener* the athletic world did not exist. His sole form of exercise was the grey constitutional round the square; and just before the closing of the gates at night, it was as if a living tube was being moved round within the wire. Five hundred odd officers were walking in couples round a square, with a circumference of four hundred yards; words cannot give an impression which can only be caught in terms of paint. For the populace billiards was the one athletic outlet.

And as the two chief resources of the average subaltern are athletics and the theatre, this suppression of one channel, diverted to the stage the entire enthusiasm of the camp. Of course each of us thinks his own little part of the world the best: our school, our company, our battalion, they seem to each individual one of us perfect

"FIVE HUNDRED ODD OFFICERS WALKING ROUND THE SQUARE."
[To face page 196.

and unique. It is only natural that we should think the P.O.W. Theatre, Mainz, the absolute Alhambra of the *Gefangenenlagers*. However bad our shows had been we should have thought them supreme. But really, considering that every costume had to be improvised, every piece of scenery painted on flimsy paper, and that female attire was unpurchasable, I do not think that its shows could have been better staged. Certainly the scenic effects towards the end of our captivity were better than anything one would have seen at a provincial pantomime, though that is in itself hardly a recommendation.

Programmes began modestly enough in the days of soup and sauerkraut. We were hungry then and had little spare vitality. But a concert party was formed that called itself the "Pows," and which gave performances every Saturday. There were many difficulties, the chief one being an entire lack of revue music. In order to get a song the aid of many had to be invoked. A committee of six would sit round a table trying to remember the words of "We've got a little Cottage" or "When Paderewski plays." Each person remembered a stray line or phrase, and gradually like a jigsaw puzzle the fabric was completed. And then the music had to be written, and luckily the "Pows" possessed in Aubrey Dowdon a musical director who could write music as fast as he could write a letter. He scored the parts, and the musician strummed them out. The result was a most amusing vaudeville performance. There were some excellent voices, romantic and humorous; Aubrey Dowdon was himself no mean vocalist, and there was Milton Hayes.

Indeed it is hard not to make the account of those early performances a mere chronicle of Milton Hayes. He was the supreme humorist. All he had to do was to stand on the stage and smile, and the audience was happy. It was a wonderful smile, that unconscious innocent affair that only childhood is supposed to know. And to watch Hayes perform was like watching a child play with bricks. It was as if he were making his jokes simply for his own pleasure, building up his toy palace of fun, and then turning to his audience to ask them how they liked it. A small stage and a small room give scope for a far deeper intimacy than is possible in the large proscenium of a London hall, where the artist can see before him only a dull blur of faces through the dusk. At Mainz Milton Hayes could see and, as it were, speak to each individual present, and before he had been on the stage five minutes one felt as if he were an old friend that one had known all one's life. He caught the true spirit of intimacy, the kindredship with his audience, that is the whole secret of the music-hall profession.

During the first two months the programme did not change much. There would be always some slight variety in a new stunt by Hayes, a new tune by Dowdon, or a topical sketch. But the old numbers continually cropped up. "The Money Moon" and "When you're a long way from Home"—these never left us. Still, they received a hearty welcome. The audience in an *Offiziergefangenenlager* is not too captious. It goes not to criticise but to be amused. And so for the first two months the "Pows" continued to entertain us every Saturday. After a while the stress of private composition caused Milton Hayes to drop out more or less, but the company went on with an undiminished vigour. And then suddenly a rumour went round the camp that a rival company was being formed, and that in a fortnight's time the "Shivers" would start their continental tour.

The general good being the one standard by which to judge any collective innovation, the enterprise of the "Shivers" must be considered the greatest benefit the camp received. Competition roused the ambition of the "Pows." Each party swore to outdo the other. There ensued a race of progressive excellence. Each performance was produced with a more lavish outlay of the public funds; each time the curtain rose a deeper gasp paid homage to scenic artists; and the composers ceased to rely for their material on the work of other men. They began to write their own songs and their own music; the old ragtime and coon melodies disappeared, and instead we had original airs and topical numbers. And here the "Pows" had a great advantage, for their musical director, who in these pages shelters himself beneath the pseudonym of Aubrey Dowdon, had a gift for libretto that we soon expect to see on the playbills of the Alhambra, and his company finally beat all records with a musical operetta entitled *The Girl on the Stairs*. All the songs were original, and it was marvellously staged. There were eastern grottos, and the gleam of white shoulders through the dusk. There was a long serenade to the Jehlum River girl, in which brown tanned slaves prostrated themselves before the half-naked form of a sylph arrayed in veils. There were humour and naughtiness, horseplay and burlesque. It was a triumph of impromptu and ingenuity, after which the activities of the "Shivers" fell woefully flat.

From the psychological standpoint the professional jealousy of those weeks of hectic rivalry provided food for much deliberation. The rivalry once definitely acknowledged, the camp did its best to foment contention. The manager of the "Shivers" would be told that, unless he was careful, he would be absolutely washed out by the "Pows," and the same story was carried to Dowdon. There were few things more amusing than to sit behind either party during a rival performance. They would simulate great enthusiasm, but all the time they would be exchanging shy and nervous glances. There would be whispers of—

"Do you think it's good?"

"Rather cheap that, isn't it?"

"What a chestnut!"

And if the piece did make a hit, what colossal "wind-up," what profound trepidation! And with what eager haste was the next show rehearsed. From the point of view of the public, this was entirely excellent. We got excellent shows, for there is no goad like jealousy.

But competition is a dangerous tool, and I often used to wonder where all this frenzy would end, and to what point it was leading. It had got beyond the well-defined limits of a good-humoured race. If it had been a case of nations, it is quite plain what the result would have been. Competition would have become contention, jealousy would have bred hatred, and there would have been a war, of which the real issue would have been, shall we say, the prop-box. But of course the companies themselves would not have fought; they had started the war, that would have been enough for them. And the ordinary *Gefangener*, who had quite unconsciously fanned this flame, by scratching at the sore place and aggravating the little itch, would find himself enrolled under one standard or the other, and involved in a war of which he was the unwitting cause.

And he would be told—well, what would he be told? That he was fighting for a prop-box? That would never do. There might come a time when he would not consider a prop-box worth the surrender of his liberty. No, the manager would have to find some striking and impersonal cause, "not for passion, or for power." A theme must be found fitting for high oratory, a framework constructed that would bear the weight of many sounding phrases. Let the poor *Gefangener* believe that he is fighting for the freedom of the English stage; let the old catchwords rip, "Art against Vulgarity," "The Drama against the Vaudeville," "Shakespeare against A Little Bit of Fluff." And then....

But fortunately we were not nations armed with a pulpit and a Press, we were simply prisoners of war, and this competition produced some very delightful entertainment. But all the same, I still wonder where things would have ended, if we had stayed there much longer. We were riding for a smash. We had exhausted our limited resources; for one man cannot compose, stage and produce a new musical comedy every fortnight, and the rivalry of the two parties had developed at such an alarming pace that we were faced with the prospect of a return to "The Money Moon," when Milton Hayes returned to the stage, and, in his own phrase, "let loose the light that set the vault of heaven on fire."

§ 2

For some weeks Milton Hayes had been living the retired life of an author, architect or other student. For he had found the effort of repeated performances in an unnatural atmosphere a very real strain on his nerves.

"No Sanatogen," he said, "that's what does it. I can't act without Sanatogen. I used to try champagne once, but it left me like a rag afterwards. Sanatogen's the stuff."

As a traveller in this commodity he would have made quite a hit. He never wearied of singing its praises, and we used to ask him why he did not forward to the firm one of those credentials that begin, "Since using your admirable tonic...."

"Why don't you try it, Milton?" we used to say. "It would be a jolly good advertisement. 'Milton Hayes, the author of the *Green Eye*, says....' You'd have your name placarded all over the kingdom."

But he would none of it.

"No," he said, "that's far too obvious. Any beginner tries that stunt, or men that are 'has beens.' I might invent a mixture. But no, not the other thing. It's not the sort of publicity one wants."

But whatever commercial advantage Sanatogen may have lacked as an advertising agent, its absence in Hayes's life certainly affected his nerves. It is a compound that he found palatable only in milk, and even condensed milk was a rare commodity. The result was that Milton Hayes joined the band of Wordsmiths in the Alcove, and spent his time working on his lyrics and on a musical comedy.

This programme satisfied him well enough for a couple of months. In France he had spent much of his time organising concert parties, and in his heart of hearts he was not sorry to be quit for a time of grease paints and the greenroom. But it could not last; and within a short time he was longing for fresh worlds to conquer. And, at the suggestion of a friend, he altered and abbreviated his musical comedy into a farcical libretto calculated to run for about a hundred minutes. This composition he laid in all good faith before the Entertainments Committee, suggesting that he should choose his cast from the pick of the "Pows" and the "Shivers," and should himself produce the show. It was a simple proposal; but he had not calculated upon the extent to which professional rivalry had imprisoned the dramatic activities of the camp.

While all the world slept momentous things had happened. A scheme of regulations had been drawn up for the guidance of the managing directors, which in a way resembled the qualifications of League Football. To prevent poaching it had been decided that, once a performer had figured on the playbills of one company, he could not transfer his allegiance elsewhere. No assistance was to be given by one party to another; only the piano, the orchestra and the prop-box were common property. There was a sort of trade boycott afoot in which only neutral waters were free from tariff.

And then into this world of regulated commerce Milton Hayes entered like the bold bad buccaneer of Romance, demanding free ports and free transport, the very pirate of legality.

Well, what the committee's opinion on this subject was, we can only conjecture. What it did is a matter of common knowledge. It absolutely refused to lend its support: why, we can but guess. Perhaps they were a little piqued at the infrequency of Hayes's appearance on the vaudeville stage; perhaps they had advanced so far into the land of tabulated orders that they could see no safe withdrawal. Perhaps.... But it is unfair to impute motives to any one. One can merely state facts, and register one's personal opinion that collectively humanity is rather stupid, and that if committees are allowed a free hand, they usually do manage to mess things up somehow; and that the conclusions at which they arrive do not at all represent the opinions of those individuals framing them.

I remember that some four and a half years ago I received a sufficiently severe beating from the School's Games Committee, on the ground that I had played roughly in a house match; and that within a week six of the seven members of that committee had apologised to me in person for their assault. This, as a testimonial to my moral worth, was no doubt comforting; but as an alleviation for the pain of those fourteen strokes, it was an inadequate recompense. And the treatment of Milton was not very different.

The committee, which consisted of ten officers, refused him their support; but each individual member of the community considered it a grave injustice, and one and all they came up to Hayes with apologies to the tune of—

"Awfully sorry, old man, about this show of yours. I wish we could have helped you. I'd love to myself, only the committee won't let me. Beastly nuisance I call it, a man isn't his own master any longer. Awfully sorry, old man."

By the time the tenth member had expressed a similar regret, Milton Hayes began to wonder whether the committee was a blind force, with a will independent of its component parts. He was naturally gratified to receive so many sympathetic condolences, but they did not materially assist him in his task of finding a company to produce his libretto. However, he beat the by-ways and hedges, and finally amassed a nondescript community, which for want of a better name he called the "Buckshees."

The company numbered thirty-two, and was supported by voluntary contribution. The "Pows" and the "Shivers" had drawn within their folds the pick of the vocalists and humorists; two dramatic societies had gleaned after them. The remaining stubble was a sorry sight, and as an insignificant member of that distinguished caste, I must confess that I viewed the first mustering of the "Buckshees" with an eye of profound misgiving. All of them were strangers to one another; and though it is easy to talk of flowers "that blow unseen," in a community such as a prison camp one is usually aware pretty early of those whom the Fates have endowed with talents. There had been little selection. Affairs had taken a course something like this. Hayes had been walking across the square when he had been accosted by a total stranger.

"I say, Hayes," he would say, "you are getting up a show or something, aren't you?"

"Yes; like a part in it?"

"Well, that's what I really came up for."

"Done any acting?"

"Oh, not much, you know, a few charades."

"Well, what do you fancy?"

"Low comedy."

"Right, then I'll put you down for the drunken slaveboy. First rehearsal to-morrow at ten in the lecture hall; thanks so much. Cheerioh."

And so the "Buckshees" were formed.

But the difficulties did not lie merely in the calibre of the artists. There was the staging, the scenery, the music. Hayes had written the songs, but who was to score the melodies? The versatile Dowdon had promised to overrule the committee and orchestrate the parts, but what of the piano? For the only two musicians had been collared by the "Pows" and the "Shivers." There were, of course, numerous strummers, but there was no composer. And it was amusing to watch the way Hayes set to work.

First of all he would write the lyric, and beat out a rhythm. He would then go and recite his composition to one Radcliffe, who could play the piano, but could not score a part; Radcliffe would get the drift of Hayes's idea, and would in the course of hours compose a harmony of sorts, which he would play to his friend Gladstone, who could score a part but could not play a piano. Gladstone would jot down the notes; and behold a finished song, the result of a sort of Progressive Whist.

The troubles of staging were less difficult. The experts had, it is true, been already commandeered by the other societies. But a serviceable quartet of carpenters was discovered, and some decorative artists procured. All these arrangements Hayes left in charge of others. He knew the art of delegating responsibility, and he certainly had his hands full with his cast. For he relied for his success on vitality, innovations, and the quality which he always dubbed as "punch." He did not ask for elaborate scenery. He knew he could not expect to equal effect of *The Girl on the Stairs*. He simply demanded an adequate setting. He would do the rest.

§ 3

With a company endowed with mediocre ability Hayes did wonders. He decided to have a beauty chorus, and with curses and entreaties he beat sixteen ungainly males into a semblance of the charm and delicacy of an Empire revue. It suffered a great deal, that chorus; it was cursed, and excommunicated. It was made a target for all the unmentionable swears. If it had been composed of girls, it would have spent half its time in tears. But eventually it emerged, in all its nudity, a machine. There was a big joyboard, running well into the auditorium; and on this it affected all the airs and graces of the courtesan. It cajoled and pleaded; it undulated with emotion. It swayed to each breath of melody, and it was not too unpleasant a sight, for Hayes had wisely transported it to an Eastern

OUR LEADING LADY.
[To face page 214.

island, to a harem, and the kindly veils of Ethiopian modesty. Through a mist of white calico it was impossible to discern the razored roughness of a cheek, and the unrazored blackness of an upper lip. The chorus was a triumph.

And the same tribute must be accorded to the leading ladies. Nature had provided them with pleasing features. Under Hayes's tuition they learnt the art of the glad eye and the droop of the lower lip. To see those beauties was to be back again in the gay world of colour and revue. A breath of femininity quivered about the rough-cast masculinity of Mainz. So much so, indeed, that on the night of the first performance a distinguished field officer, who had drunk deeply not only of romance, was observed chasing round the corridor behind the flying feet of an inclement Venus, and murmuring between his gasps, "Don't call me Major, call me Jim"; and even the most hardened misogynists were not unconscious of a thrill when "Leola," the daughter of the Hesperides, tripped down the joyboard, and sang with outspread, enticing arms, that beckoned to the audience—

"Come to Sonalia with me."

The plot of the play was extravagantly simple. The curtain went up, revealing a harassed author searching among his papers for a hidden plot. The show was billed to start at two o'clock, but the play was lost, what should he do? And then the machinery of Romance began. An Arabic inscription gave the key. "Why should they not wish for the plot?" Faith would remove mountains, and Faith caused to emerge from the back of the stage a green-faced being, who called himself "The King of Wishland."

From then onwards it was plain sailing: the barrier between the phenomenal and the real was torn aside, and we were in the world of fancy. And it was no surprise when this obliging monarch produced a strange device which he called a "thoughtoscope," through which could be observed the hurried arrival from New York of the Financier who was to find a plot. Through this mendacious lens we saw him cross from Halifax to London. He was in an aeroplane, he was over Holland, he was coming down the Rhine, he had landed in Mainz, and look, amid gigantic enthusiasm the gates of the theatre were flung open and Milton Hayes, disguised as Silas P. Hawkshaw, was observed charging across the square, waving a stick and a suitcase.

What followed was sheer joy. The company rose to the occasion. With perfect equanimity we received the news that, in order to find the plot, we should have to be transported to Wishland. In Silas P. Hawkshaw we placed a blind unquestioning trust, and before we knew where we were, the curtain was down, and the chorus was regaling the audience, while the scene-shifters did their noble work.

When next the curtain rose it revealed a tropical island splashed in sunshine. Through a vista of palms gleamed the azure stretches of some ultimate shoreless sea. But no one would have willingly set sail. The island was too full of charm. There were singing girls and dancing girls, a sultan's harem, and an American bar, and the story lost itself in a riot of intrigue. The plot abandoned all coherence. It was a fairy dream, in which a magic ring changed hands innumerable times, involving disastrous loves and deserted widows.

And through all this medley of incidents Hayes wandered, first in one garb, then in another. As a Scotsman he swallowed whisky, as a Welshman took two wives, as a padre wandered into a harem, and as "Leda was the mother of Helen of Troy, and all this was to him but as the sound of lyres and flutes." It was for him a great triumph, and perhaps the most supreme moment was, when he proffered marriage to a much-married widow, and suggested that they should spend their holiday in a bungalow, in a duet of which the first verse is too good to be forgotten—

LIEUT. MILTON HAYES, M.C. AS SILAS P. HAWKSHAW.
[To face page 218.

"*He.* How'd you like a Bungalow for two, dear?

She. How'd you like to furnish it complete?

He. It would be a cosy nest, dear.

Like the grey home in the west, dear.

She. And on Sunday I should let you cook the meat,

He. We'd have a little bedroom made for two, dear,

She. A little bed, a little chair or so;

He. And in a month or two, it maybe,

　　We should have a little baby

Both. Grand piano in our Bungalow."

There were four more verses, in the main topical, and the play ran its way through the complete gamut of upheavals, matrimonial and domestic. It was impossible to tell who was allied to whom. It was a complete and utter socialism, and even the great Plato himself would have been satisfied with that community of wives.

But it had to end; and, to carry the spirit of burlesque to its conclusion, we finished with a pantomime procession. The chorus came on, as choruses always do, in couples beating time with their heels. And in their hands they brandished banners on which were inscribed the names nearest to the northern heart, "Preston," "Wigan," "Johnnie Walker," "Steve Bloomer." Then the protagonists appeared, each with an appropriate tag, the lovers with a curtsey and a bow—

"And so through every kind of weather
We two will always cling together."

The gay lady still naughtily impenitent—

"Although I haven't chanced to find a feller,
I crave your pity; pity poor Finella."

The evil genie of the piece, his brows wrinkled with gloom—

"You see my work I never shirk,
For I've done all the dirty work."

And, last of all, Milton Hayes with a wand, a simper and a skirt—

"Without my aid where would poor Jack have been?
So please reward the little fairy queen."

And after that was sung once again the opening chorus, and the curtain was rung down on the most enjoyable show of the P.O.W. Theatre, Mainz, which by a strange and lucky coincidence also happened to be the last. For within a day or two the armistice was signed, and the companies and committees were scattered. It remains now for Milton Hayes to give once more to London audiences the pleasure that he gave to us. But because sentiment lies so near to the human heart, I think his association with the "Buckshees" will recall to Milton Hayes more pleasant memories than those of his other and perhaps more universal successes. At a time when life was grey and tedious, he provided us with interest, with employment and amusement. We can only hope that he enjoyed himself as much as we did.

CHAPTER XIII

ARMISTICE DAYS

§ 1

SINCE my return, so many people have asked me whether prisoners of war had any idea of the turn affairs were taking during the autumn, that it would be as well to state here exactly what our sources of information were. There were only two papers printed in English, the *Anti-Northcliffe Times* and the *Continental Times*. The former I never saw, and it cannot have had a very large circulation. But the *Continental Times*, which appeared three times a week, was to be found in every room in the camp. It was the most mendacious chronicle. It was printed at Berlin, and was published solely for British prisoners of war; a more foolish production can hardly be imagined. Its views, political and military, changed with each day's tidings, and its chief object was to impress on British prisoners the relative innocence of Germany and perfidy of the Entente. But it was so badly done that it can never have achieved its ends. It was far too violent, and so obviously partial. Its only interesting features were the reproductions from the English weeklies of articles by men like Ivor Brown and Bertrand Russell; once they even paid me the doubtful honour of a quotation, a tribute considerably enhanced by the appearance of the poem under the name of Siegfried Sassoon.

But no one took the *Continental Times* seriously, and the paper that we relied on for our news was the *Frankfurter Zeitung*, the representative organ of the Rhine towns. There were two issues daily. The morning one contained the Alliance *communiqués*, and the evening one the Entente. Like all other German papers, it was under the strictest censorship of the military bureaucrats, but it maintained nevertheless an extraordinary impartiality. It rarely indulged in heroics, and except for a little "hot air" on March 22nd it kept its head remarkably well. It is, of course, the most moderate paper in the country, and the *Berliner Tageblatt* is considerably more hectic. But the *Frankfurter Zeitung* was, certainly during the period of my captivity, more restrained than any British daily publication. It can be most fittingly compared, in tone though not in politics, with our sixpenny weekly papers whose appeal is to the educated classes.

From this paper we could get a pretty fair idea of how things were going; but even without the paper we should have been prepared for the debacle of November. For we could see what the papers do not show—and that is the psychology of the people. For so long their hopes had been buoyed up by the expectations of immediate victories in the field; they had been told that the March offensive would most surely bring them this peace; and on this belief had rested their entire faith. For this they had maintained a war that was crippling them. They had endured sufferings greater than those of either France or England. Their casualties had been colossal, the civilian population had been starved. But yet they had hung on, because they had been told that victory would bring them peace; and then Foch attacked; their expectations were overthrown; the Entente were still fresh and ready to fight. There was talk of unlimited resources, and Germany was faced with the prospect of a long and harassing war that could end only in exhaustion and reverse; and that the German people were not prepared to endure.

For there will always come a point at which the individual will refuse to have his interests sacrificed for a collective abstraction with which he has not identified himself. Mankind in the mass has neither mind nor memory, and can be swayed and blinded by a clever politician; it can be led to the brink of folly without realising what road it follows. Collectively it is capable of injustice which in an individual it would never countenance; but sooner or later the collective emotion yields before the personal demand, and the individual asks himself, "Why am I doing this? Am I benefiting from it; and if I am not benefiting from it, who is?" For, of course, by even the most successful war the position of the individual is not improved. The indemnities and confiscations that the treaty brings never cover the expenses and privations previously entailed. And collective honour is perishable stuff. But as long as the war is successful, the politicians are able to persuade the people that they are actually gaining something from it. They can say, "We have got this island and that; here our frontier has been pushed forwards, and in return for that small concession, look, behold an indemnity." And because mankind has neither mind nor memory it is prepared to forget the millions of pounds that had to be spent first, and the quantity of blood that had to be spilt.

That is when the war is successful; but when defeat looms near, whatever the courtly ministers may urge, the individual will contrast in his own mind the ravages, that another two years of warfare will entail, with the possible emoluments that may lie at the end of them. He will say to himself, "It is reasonable to expect that, by fighting for another two years, we may eventually get better terms than we should get now, if we signed a peace. But to me personally, is the difference sufficient to warrant the sufferings of a protracted war?" And the answer, as often as not, is "No." That is, as far as one can judge, the sort of argument that presented itself to the individual German in the weeks following Foch's resumption of the attack. And in determining the forces that went to the framing of that "no," the most important thing to realise is that Germany was actually starving.

That this is so, a certain portion of the Press has, during the last month, attempted to deny; and it is rumoured that the armies of occupation have found the German towns well stocked with food. If this last report is true, I do not profess to be able to explain it; but of one thing there can be no doubt, while we were prisoners in Mainz the German people there were not merely hungry, they were starving. It is true that meat was obtainable in restaurants, but only at a price so high as to be well beyond the means of even the moderately wealthy. A dinner, consisting of a plate of soup and a plate of meat and vegetables, would in places cost as much as twelve to fifteen marks, and the majority of men and women had to exist entirely on their rations. Of many of the necessaries of life it was impossible to get enough, especially in the case of butter and milk and cheese. Of meat there was very little, and flour could only be bought at an exorbitant price. The bread ration was small, and eggs were rarely obtainable. Potatoes alone were plentiful, and two years of such a diet had considerably lowered the nation's vitality.

In times of sickness this weakness produced heavy fatalities, especially among the children. A German father even went to the lengths of offering an English officer a hundred marks for a shilling packet of chocolate to give to his son who was sick. And all the children born during the last two years are miserably weak and puny; some of them even having no nails on their toes and fingers.

"You are not a father, so you will not understand," a German soldier said to me. "But it is a most terrible thing to watch, as I have watched during the last four years, a little boy growing weaker and paler month after month; and I can tell you that when I look at my little boy, all that I want is that this war should end, I do not care how."

And it is only natural that the individual parent should feel like this, and I do not think that in England we quite realise all that Germany has suffered. I remember one morning after the signing of the armistice that some small boys of about seven years old climbed up the outside of the citadel, and asked us for some food. We gave them a few biscuits; they were very hard and dry, but I have never seen such excitement and joy on a child's face before. It was a most pathetic sight. A child of that age cannot feign an emotion, and those children were absolutely starving.

And the knowledge that this was so must have had a very saddening effect on the German soldier at the front. For one of the very few consolations that were granted to a British soldier in the line was the certainty that his wife and family were well and safe. But the German soldier must have been faced continually with the thought that, whatever sufferings he might himself endure, he could not protect those he loved from the hunger that was crushing them, and for him those long cold nights and lonely watches must have been unrelieved by any gleam of hope.

It is not natural that any nation should bear such hardships for an instant longer than they appeared absolutely needful, and when it became quite clear that the Entente had not only survived the March offensive, but had emerged from it with undiminished powers, the Germans began to agitate for an instant peace. At the beginning they were not aware of their weakness in the field, and when the first armistice note was sent the terms expected were very light.

"We shall probably have to evacuate France and Belgium," they said, "and perhaps Italy and Palestine. That's all the guarantee that will be required."

And at this point, as far as we could gather, there was very little animosity against the Kaiser.

"Of course," they said, "this sort of thing must not happen again. We shall have to tie him down a good deal. Ministers will have to be responsible to the Reichstag and not to him. That should ensure us."

There was hardly any talk of a republic.

But when the Austrian and Bulgarian armies crumpled up, and Foch began to threaten invasion from every side, it was as if a sort of panic seized the Germans. They felt that they must have an armistice at any cost, and were terribly afraid it would not be granted them. They thought that the French would demand revenge for every indignity and injustice they had suffered in 1871; and when they realised that the Entente was not prepared to treat with the Kaiser, they clamoured for his abdication. It was an ignoble business. Even the *Frankfurter Zeitung* joined in the tumult. There was a general terror which gave birth to the revolution.

§ 2

The revolutionists arrived at Mainz on Friday, November 8th, and the first intimation we received of their presence was the arrival on morning parade of the German adjutant in a civilian suit. He had apparently spent the previous evening at Köln, where all officers had been advised either to leave the town as speedily as possible, or else change into mufti. This gallant officer did both, and for the first time since we were captured, we were dismissed without an *appel*.

During the whole of that day the camp was possessed of rumours. At any moment we were told the revolutionaries might present themselves before the gates; we should be in their hands; our whiskered sentries would have neither the power nor the inclination to protect us. Thoughts of

Bolshevism worked disquietingly within our minds; we pictured a sanguinary contest between the military and socialist parties, and we were a little nervous lest the caprice of the moment should ally us with one or other of the warring parties. The town was clearly under the power of the Red Flag. German officers were not allowed in the streets in uniform, and it was a pleasant sight to see the General robing himself in a suit of mustard-coloured cloth before venturing beyond the gate. But I must own that personally I was considerably alarmed about my safety. However deep-rooted may be one's objections to constitutions and their rulers, however much one may sympathise with the ἰδέα of rebellion, one does prefer to view these calamitous upheavals either from the safety of a hearthrug, or from a distance of two hundred yards.

And it seemed more than likely that, on the signing of the armistice, we should have to beat a very hasty retreat which would involve the dumping of the greater part of our kit; and we had received no information of what we might take with us. This was very disquieting. During the eight months of my confinement I had written some two-thirds of a novel, and had no wish to discover that manuscript was contraband. Tarrant viewed my troubles with complete composure.

"My dear Waugh," he said, "as I've told you more than once before, that novel is quite unprintable, and if it is published, it will plunge both you and your publisher into disaster. You'd do much better to leave it here."

But with this I could naturally not agree, and in a state of some perturbation carried my heart-searchings to the German adjutant. He received me most affectionately.

"Ah, Mr. Waugh," he said, "things are not as serious as all that. It will be all right. If, of course, you had been exchanged, it would have been a different thing. But now you can take what you like, and I am sure that anything you write would be quite harmless."

"Quite harmless".... I thought of all the scholastic fury that had been split over Gordon Carruthers, I thought of Mr. Dames-Longworth who had called it "pernicious" stuff, of Canon Lyttelton who had spoken so much and to such little purpose, and who had given me so royal an advertisement. And I thought of that long stream of correspondents who had signed themselves "A mere schoolmaster," and I thought of what they will say of my new book if it ever sees the light of day; and it seemed to me that of all the adjectives both of appreciation and abuse that may be attached to that sorry work, "harmless" is certainly the one it will never receive again.

During the remainder of the day rumours bred at an alarming pace. It was reported that the revolutionaries had taken charge of the camp, and that although the armistice was still unsigned, they had told us to make our own arrangements about repatriation. Already negotiations had been opened with a shipping firm that was to take us down the Rhine to the Dutch frontier. We had visions of England within a week.

As to the state of affairs in the town only conjecture was possible; but from the top windows of Block II, the slate roofs presented the same somnolent appearance, and it was hard to realise that beneath that placid landscape Democracy was lighting its flaming torch.

Most of our information came from the medical orderly. In pre-war days he had been a waiter at the Carlton, and he had not forgotten how to swear in English. He was one of the most complete terrorists.

"Europe is overrun with Bolshevism," he said. "It is everywhere. You have it in England. Do you know that you have soldiers' councils in England? You have. Did you know that the British Fleet sailed into Kiel Harbour flying the Red Flag? It did. Soon the whole world will be having revolutions. There will be no safety, none at all."

He was most hectic, and on the day of the armistice his anger exceeded all bounds.

"Why do you give us terms like this?" he said. "We have got rid of our roundheads, our Kaiser, our Ludendorf. Why do you not get rid of yours? Ah, but Bolshevism will come, and do you know what your soldiers' councils have done, they have wired to us not to sign the armistice. But the wire came too late. Still, it will be all right in time, your soldiers' councils will see to that."

Where the Germans got the idea that there were soldiers' councils in England, I do not know. It certainly did not appear in the *Frankfurter Zeitung*. But an enormous number of Germans were under the impression that a corresponding state of affairs existed in England. Probably it was a point of the revolutionaries' programme.

By November 11th the revolution, as far as Mainz was concerned, had more or less adjusted itself; and the people's attention was so occupied by the new regime that the news of the armistice was not received with as much excitement as might have been expected. The terms were a great deal harder than they had hoped for, but they were so glad the war was over that this did not greatly trouble them. They had ceased to care for collective honour. The only man I met who was really conscious of the defeat was the professor who used to take French and German classes. Of course, all his life it had been his business to instil imperialistic propaganda into the boys and girls under him, and no doubt he himself must have considerably absorbed the Pan-German doctrines, and he did feel acutely the ignominy of his country's position.

"What hurts our pride more than anything else," he said, "is the thought that we release prisoners instead of exchanging them. It shows us so clearly that we are beaten."

But the people themselves were not at all worried about this. The only thing that troubled them was the doubt whether they would be able to get enough to eat after the surrender of so many wagons. The grippe was raging very fiercely among them, and the need for food was being very keenly felt. They had also hoped that one of the conditions of the armistice would have been the removal of the blockade.

"You have beaten us," they said. "We cannot fight any more. Why must you continue the blockade? We have done everything you asked for; the Kaiser has gone; we have a new Government."

For they have not yet realised the extent to which the previous deceit of their military rulers has discredited them in the eyes of Europe. They do not realise that every political movement they make has come to be regarded with suspicion.

With us the revolution produced fewer ludicrous situations than it did in some other places, and a most amusing story is told about the camp at Frankfurt. A few days after the signing of the armistice the senior British officer and his adjutant presented themselves before the German Commandant, with the request that they might be allowed out in the town on parole. There they found their late tyrant, sitting down in his shirt-sleeves, cutting the epaulettes off his tunic. On their arrival, however, he put on his greatcoat and made an attempt to recover his dignity.

"Yes, gentlemen," he said, with his courtly foreign grace.

The senior British officer explained his errand. "As we're no longer prisoners," he said, "we may surely go out for walks?"

The German looked a little awkward.

"Well," he said hesitatingly, "the fact is, I really am not the person to ask. You see, the soldiers' council are in command. You must go and ask Herr Bomenheim, he is the representative."

And besides being representative of the revolution, Herr Bomenheim was also the window cleaner; it is a strange world in which a colonel takes his orders from his batman.

At Mainz we were less democratic, as our affairs were run by a sergeant-major. But for all that we had no truck with the old regime, and the "Soldaten Raht" proved its independence by court-martialling the Prussian General. For that deed alone the prisoners of Mainz bear to the revolutionaries a debt of everlasting gratitude. And the escapade that led to this retribution provides a fitting example of all that is most aggressive and inhuman in the Berlin military caste.

At this time there was a very great deal of sickness in Mainz, and the hospitals were crowded both with civilians and British officers. It was also a time at which congestion of the railroads had delayed the arrival of our Red Cross parcels. The British authorities in the camp had in consequence collected as large a supply of food as possible, to be sent to the hospital and divided not only among our own invalids, but among those of the civilian population whose condition was really critical. This consignment was loaded on a handcart, and surrounded, by sentries, was to proceed into the town.

At the gates, however, it was met by the General, who, by the courtesy of the revolutionaries, was now allowed to wear his uniform. He immediately stopped the handcart and asked where it was going; on being informed of its destination he ordered that the food should be returned at once to the officers who had collected it, as he could in no wise countenance such a proceeding. It was pointed out to him that the condition of several officers in the hospital was most serious, and that meat stuffs were urgently required. But he would have none of it.

"My permission was not asked first," he said, "and I cannot allow it. If you had come to me, it would have been different. But I cannot have you behaving as though you were under your own rule."

And it is to the credit of the soldiers' council that they took instant steps in the matter. The General was informed that he only occupied his position on tolerance and had no active authority whatsoever. And within two days he was removed from the camp, and is now, I believe, awaiting court-martial on a charge of "inhumanity and callousness."

And all the while rumours about our release bred at an alarming rate. The German authorities had told us that it would be impossible for them to provide us with a train for at least a fortnight, but that if we liked we could make our own arrangements, and charter a steamer that would take us up the Rhine. These were days of furious conjecture. The complete technique of a pleasure trip was exhaustively discussed. How long did it take a steamer to coal? how long to get up steam? And then of how many knots an hour was it capable? Sums were worked out on the old methods of, Let x be the rate of the steamer, and y the speed of the Rhine. We roughly gauged that it would take twenty-seven hours. But then, of course, the Dutch Government had to be considered. However delightful we might be as individual companions, we were not at all sure whether a neutral country would welcome the sudden arrival of 500 guests. Of course they had received the Kaiser, but that was not quite the same thing. There was an inconvenient margin of doubt.

It was a most disquieting time. Each hour was filled with conflicting rumours, and after a while one ceased to believe in any of them. We assumed that on the arrival of the army of occupation we should be liberated, and it appeared as if we should have to wait till then.

On November 17th, however, we were given an official permit to go into the town, and from then onwards the burden of waiting was light.

CHAPTER XIV

FREEDOM

§ 1

AFTER a confinement of eight months it was a wonderful thing to be able to walk through the streets unguarded. To be free again; no longer to be fenced round by barbed wire, to be shadowed by innumerable eyes; no longer to be under the rule of an arrogant Prussian. It was almost impossible to grasp it; that we were free, free. Every moment I expected to feel a heavy hand fall on my shoulder, and to hear a gruff voice bellow in my ear, "Es ist verboten, Herr Lieutenant."

And this sense of unreality was increased by our reception outside the gates. Whether the children had been given a half-holiday in honour of their recent naval operations, I do not know, but it did seem as though the entire infantile population had assembled outside the citadel; and no sooner did an officer appear than he was surrounded by urchins of both sexes, up to the age of twelve, all yelling for biscuits and chocolate. It was an absurd and pitiable sight; and it was terrible to think that a people had so far lost their self-respect as to allow their children to beg for food from their enemies. It was often quite hard to get rid of them; they would hang on to an arm or to the end of a coat, and simply refuse to let go till actually forced.

Considering that the nation, of which it formed a part, had just sustained a defeat practically amounting to unconditional surrender, Mainz presented a spectacle of strange jubilation. I had expected to find an atmosphere of a more or less passive resignation, of disappointment only partially relieved by the cessation of hostilities; whatever the individual might feel, officialdom surely, we had thought, would assume a woeful countenance. But instead of that we found a town robed as for a carnival. Flags were hung from the windows of every house, the children in the streets waved penny ensigns, and every few minutes a lorry full of troops would clatter through, the guns decked with banners, the men shouting and singing. It was as though a victorious army were returning home, and after all it was only right that the men should receive a proper welcome. For over four years they had waged on many fronts a war that had conferred much honour on their arms. They had been at all times brave and resolute. They had fought to the very end. It was not their fault that Germany had been steeped in ruin.

The reception we received from the civil population was very friendly. At first it was only with the most extreme diffidence that we entered cafés and restaurants, but we soon saw that there was little or no animosity against us. In the streets civilians were always ready to show us the way, and displayed no resentment at our presence amongst them. In the cafés German soldiers even came up and spoke to us. There was such general delight at the war being over, that the Germans felt it impossible to harbour any ill-will against any save those whom they held directly responsible for their sufferings, and it was typical of their attitude that, when a German soldier introduced himself, his first remark was, "I am not a Prussian."

The question of the army of occupation was very keenly discussed, and everywhere was to be found the same opinion, "We do not want the French." It seemed as if that hereditary hate was as keen as ever; for the English and Americans they entertained very neutral emotions. But the French were too nearly neighbours; and it seems as if only the long passage of uneventful years could assuage this spirit of vindictiveness, that has been artificially fostered in the nursery and in the schoolroom.

But between us and the Germans, at any rate in the Southern States, there is no reason why this hate should outlive the war. That is, of course, if the attitude of the people of Mainz can be taken as in any way representative of the other Rhine towns. For we could not have been more hospitably received. There are those, of course, who will say, "Ah, but they were pulling your leg, they were only trying to see what they could get out of you. You spent money in their cafés, that was what they wanted; and you gave them chocolate and soup, that's what they were after." I have not the slightest doubt that a great many Germans attached themselves to us solely for ulterior purposes. But as a whole I believe that the civilians in Mainz were quite honestly pleased to be able to do for us anything they could, as a sort of proof that they had altered their Government, that the war was over, and that they had no wish to nourish any ill-feeling against us. And those who see behind this display of friendship the calculated deceit of a political stunt, are, it seems to me, merely seeing their own reflections in the looking-glass of life.

The Germans themselves were immensely enthusiastic about the revolution; they saw in it a complete social panacea.

"Everything will be all right now," one of them said to me. "We shall abolish our big standing army, and our big fleet, and so we shall be able to cut down our taxes. Before the war our lives were being crushed out of us, so that generals could retire on large pensions. But now every one will have to work. We shall be really democratic."

"And," he said, "we are not going to have our children overworked in the schools. We shall cut down the hours. Before, it was so hard to earn a living in Germany, that children had to work like that or they would have been left behind. Competition was ruining us. But now...."

There was there the blind optimism that is born by the glimmering of a hope however far withdrawn. The only real dread they had was that, when the troops returned, Bolshevism might break out.

"You see," he went on, "at the front the troops were well fed. Of course they had no delicacies, but they had enough; while now they are returning to a country that is practically starving. They will have to share with us; we are no longer militarists, and we do not see why they should have the best of everything. It is possible that there will be trouble. But whatever we do, we shall not be like Russia. We have more common sense, we are better educated, we are not religious maniacs, we shall not be swayed by a few demagogues. We are too sane to go to such extremities."

And it was quite clear that they had no intention of restoring the Kaiser. Having once decided to choose him as their scapegoat, they had done the business thoroughly. On him they laid the whole burden of their adversities.

"He led us into this, and he kept the truth from us. If we had known that it would come to this, we would have made peace months ago. We should not have let our children die for want of food."

But, as regards actual liberty, the revolution had merely substituted one tyranny for another, and that a military one. No doubt things will adjust themselves shortly, and at this time strong discipline was clearly essential. But the individual had very little freedom. The patrols of the Red Guard paraded the streets all day with loaded rifles; at eleven o'clock they entered and cleared the cafés. After that hour they arrested any one they found in the streets. Moreover, they had authority to raid private houses whenever they liked, a privilege of which they frequently availed themselves. Altogether this government of the people by the people did not seem to me so desirable an Utopia, though as a revolution it might be a triumph of order and moderation.

Our week of liberty in Mainz passed quickly and pleasantly. It was a coloured, leisured life, a continual drifting from one café to another; we played innumerable games of billiards, listened to the music in the Kaiserhof, sampled all the cinemas, and heard *Der Troubadour* at the theatre. Just off the main street was a small restaurant where we took all our meals. It was in rather an out-of-the-way spot, and as we were the only officers to discover it, we became during that week a sort of institution. The proprietor struck up quite a friendship with us, and whenever we came in, he used to produce from his cupboard a bottle of tomato sauce. It bore the name of

Crosse & Blackwell, and he was very proud of his possession. To offer us a share in it was the greatest compliment he could pay.

Our last night there I shall never forget. We came in rather late for dinner, and by the time we had finished it was well after ten, but the proprietor insisted on us staying a little longer. He set us down at the same table as his friends and produced a vast quantity of wine. They were hospitable folk, and two hours' companionship over a bottle had removed all tendencies to reserve.

Opposite me was a German officer who had spent the greater part of his life in England; and his flow of words bore irrefutable testimony to the potency of Rhine wine.

"I have lived among you all my life," he said; "I do not wish to fight against you. I have no quarrel with the English. It is only the French I hate, the bloody French. I would do anything I could to harm them. They hate us and we hate them," and a man generally speaks the truth when he is drunk.

The end of the evening was less glorious. It was well after eleven before we managed to escape after countless *Aufwiedersehens*, and no sooner had we got outside the house than we walked straight into a patrol of the Red Guard, by whom we were arrested, and returned to the citadel under an armed escort.

Next morning we were marched down into a train for Metz. All the German officers from the camp and a considerable number of civilians came to see us off. As I leant out of the window, to catch a last glimpse of the cathedral, it was hardly possible to realise that the war was over and that we were going home. It was the day to which we had looked forward for so long, the day of which we had dreamt so much during the cold and loneliness of the nights in France. It had been then immeasurably remote, a flickering uncertain gleam, too far away for any tangible hope. And the mind had fastened upon those nearer probabilities of leave,—a blighty, or a course behind the line. And now that day had really come, I could not grasp its significance. I was almost afraid to look forward, and my mind went back to the earlier days of our captivity, to the hunger and the depression, to the intolerable tedium and irritation. And yet, for all that, a wave of sentimentality partially obscured the sharpness of those memories. We had had some good times there in the citadel; that grey monochrome had not been entirely unrelieved. There had been certain moments worth remembering; and I thought that, when the incidents of the past four years had settled down into their true perspective, I should be able to look back, not without a certain kindliness, towards that unnatural life, that strange world of substitute and sauerkraut.

§ 2

The journey home was protracted by innumerable delays. We left Mainz on November 24th, and it was not until the 5th of December that we arrived in London. We spent five days in Nancy, another three in Boulogne, and the trains behaved as is their wont on the railroads of France. All this rather tended to dispel the glamour of the return.

For one of the chief attractions of leave is its suddenness. One is sitting on the steps of a dugout musing gloomily on the probable chance of a relief, when a runner arrives from Battalion with a chit, "You will proceed on U.K. leave to-night. The train leaves Arras at 8.10 p.m." And then the world is suddenly haloed with flame. One rushes down the dugout, flings hurried orders to the sergeant, collects all that is least important in one's kit, scatters an extravagance of largess among the batmen who have collected it, and then races for H.Q. It is all a scramble and a rush. The mess cart is chartered, within a couple of hours one is at the railhead; a night of cramp and discomfort and one is at Boulogne; there is just time for a bath at the E.F.C. Club, and then the boat sails. There is a train waiting at the other end, and the whole business takes only twenty-four hours. It is like a tale from the *Arabian Nights*. At one moment one is sitting on a firestep, the next one is in London. It embodies the very essence of romance.

But the return of the *Gefangener* was altogether different. He had plenty of time in which to collect his thoughts, the return to civilised life was marked by slow gradations. At Metz he could get a decent bath, at Nancy a decent dinner. By the time he had reached Boulogne, his odyssey had assumed the most prosaic proportions. There is no doubt about it, for those who had been prisoners only a few months the leave boat was infinitely more exciting.

But there were, of course, compensations. After having lived on tinned meats for eight months, it was a thrilling experience to find a menu that comprised fried sole and grouse, Brussel sprouts and iced grapes. Over my first dinner I took three hours. It was a gluttonous but on the whole a natural exhibition. It also saved us from a further period of confinement.

For when we arrived at Nancy one of the first pieces of intelligence we received, was the news that it would not be possible to provide a train for us within five days. To many ardent spirits this was a sad blow, and one or two adventurers decided that whatever the rest might do, they themselves were not going to wait five days "for any blooming train," and among these rebels I had rather naturally numbered myself.

During the afternoon I went down to the station with Barron, the constant companion of my peradventures, and interviewed the railway authorities. Now there is only one way to deal with a military policeman; it is no good trying to dodge him. He knows that trick too well. The frontal assault is the one road to success. We walked straight up to him.

"Corporal," I said, "we're going to Paris."

"Very good, Sir; you've got your movement order made out, I suppose."

"No, Corporal, I'm afraid I haven't," I confessed.

He grunted.

"That makes it a bit awkward, Sir; you see, I have got orders, Sir, to...."

At this juncture a five-franc note changed hands.

"But, Sir, of course it could be managed, I expect, if you're down at ten minutes to eleven. Well, Sir, I'll see what I can do."

That was all right; and feeling ourselves rather dogs, we made our way back to the Stanislas and had a game of billiards. At half-past six we sat down to a long, carefully selected dinner and two bottles of champagne; and as the evening progressed a delightful warmth and languor came over us. A bed with a spring mattress seemed more than ever desirable.

"It won't be a very comfortable journey," hazarded my companion. "It will take a good ten hours."

"Yes," I said.

"It really seems rather a sweat...."

"Old man," I said sternly, "I've paid that corporal five francs, and on my mother's side I'm Scots."

And we returned to our attack on the omelette.

Half an hour passed, and the world of languor grew even fairer. Effort then appeared almost criminal. Surely the supreme delight of life lay in this slow puffing at a cigarette. The idea of our all-night journey became increasingly abhorrent.

"Archie," I said, "do you think we shall be able to get any sleep in this train?"

"We shall be too cold. You know what a French train is?"

And again there was a silence. By this time we had reached the coffee stage. In about half an hour we should have to go. There would be a longish walk back to our billets, then we should have to pack and lug our bags all the way down to the station. It really didn't seem worth while....

"Look here," I said, "we shall only gain five days by this, and I'm jolly sleepy...."

"And if it's your Scots blood that is troubling you," my companion burst out, "I'll pay you the damned five francs now, and with interest."

That settled it.

"Garçon," I called, "l'addition, s'il vous plaît, et cherchez-moi un fiacre, je suis fort épuisé."

But the others were either made of sterner stuff, or else they had wearied of the lures of the Stanislas. At any rate they presented themselves duly before the military policeman at 10.50, and a quarter of an hour later they were on their way to Paris, to that city of gay colours and gayer women; while stretched out peacefully on a delightful spring mattress, two renegades slept a coward's sleep.

Well, the last I heard of those lambent rebels was that on their arrival at Paris they were instantly arrested by the A.P.M., and when we left Boulogne they were still sending urgent telegrams over France, begging for an instant release. Whether this has been since accorded them I do not know, but when I went down to Victoria a week after my arrival to meet a friend, I saw, stacked in a neglected corner, a huge pile of the white wood boxes that were peculiar to the Offiziergefangenenlager, Mainz. And on those boxes were the names of those bright warriors who had defied authority. Their luggage had come on afterwards with us, and had preceded them by many days. They were very gallant fellows, very resolute and proud-hearted, but ... I am glad I went to the Stanislas.

And when we did eventually move from Nancy, it was not in one of the unspeakable leave trains, but in a hospital train, fitted with every possible convenience and comfort. As in the haven of the Pre-Raphaelite, there were "beds for all who come," and beds, moreover, that were poised on springs, and that swung gently to the movement of the engine. For thirty-six hours we slept solidly.

And at Boulogne we were provided with a hospital boat; indeed, we might have been the most serious stretcher cases, instead of being rather untidy, very lazy, and thoroughly war-weary *Gefangenen*. It was a royal return.

Twenty-four hours later, with a warrant for two months' leave in my pocket, I was standing on Victoria platform, a free man. I had often wondered what it would feel like. Would it seem very strange to be no longer under authority, to be able to do what I liked, and to go where I wanted? I had wondered whether the atmosphere of a prison camp would still hang over me, and whether I should see in commissionaires and waiters some dim survival of those whiskered sentries. When I went to a theatre, should I turn rather nervously to the powdered lackey in the vestibule, as if half expecting a thundered "es ist verboten"? Would it take long to drop those habits of subservience?

But when I was once there, all those misgivings were as a dream. It seemed that I had never been away at all. With my old-time skill, I overawed a taxi-driver, and promised to "make it worth his while." I drove round to my banker, and cashed an enormous cheque; then to my tailors to order a civilian suit. And then—Hampstead.

I lay back against the padded cushion and watched each well-known landmark fall behind me—Lord's, Swiss Cottage, the Hampstead cricket field. Surely I had never been away at all. Those eight months in Germany, they were merely some old remnant of a fairy tale, *ein Märchen aus alten Zeiten*; they had no real existence. I felt as though I were coming back from Sandhurst for my Christmas leave. There had been no separation. In the last month I had had one week-end leave and two Sunday passes. It was just a resumption of the old life, a slipping back into the ordered harmony of days.

The taxi drew up outside the door; I knocked on the window with my stick, and the hall was instantly alive with welcome. But I could not make it an occasion for heroics. It did not seem in any way a special event, demanding any exceptional excitement.

"Father," I said, "I've got no change. You might give that taxi-driver ten shillings."

9 789362 516831